On my Way

An intimate journey along St James' Way

Martin Knapp

ISBN-13: 9798605269052

For Thomas and Eloïse

Contents

Acknowledgments

My thanks go to my friend Florence, who encouraged me during my journey, and whose letters contributed to this little book. They go to Amaïa who welcomed me in Bilbao and revealed the city to me. They go to all the volunteer *hospitaleros* who look after the hostels and *albergues* on the Camino, and without whom the journey would have been much more arduous. They go to all those that I met as I walked, whether pilgrims or not, whose thoughts, company, and conversation have enriched my life.

Last but not least, my thanks go to you, gentle reader, for your interest and even more for your indulgence. This book was originally written in French which is not my mother tongue. I had thought that it would be easy enough to translate it into English, but it seems that *"traduttore, traditore"*, as the Italians say, to translate is to betray, holds good even when you are translating your own words into your own native language. I have no doubt that some of the expressions I have used are less than felicitous. Finally, the whole thing was written, typed, translated, corrected, laid out and published by one person working alone. Inevitably and despite my best efforts, errors will have crept in.

It is customary at this point in a book to say that "any mistakes are my own", but in this case that really goes without saying.

Go, yes. But where?

Writing is born of an illusion: the illusion that I am better than I really am, more penetrating, more generous and more sensitive. The illusion also, that I am capable of writing.
Nicolas Bouvier, *Le vide et le plein*

I hadn't really intended to go to Compostela.

It was 2016, and I was due to retire the following year. From time to time, various official bodies would send me advice on how to organise my life as a future retiree, which I ignored. Just the word irritated me, as if society in general were inviting me to "withdraw". You can feel it in the economists' jargon: I was no longer to be part of the "active workforce" . Well, think again gentlemen, I said to myself, I may no longer be at work, but I intend to be much more active in retirement than I was stuck behind a computer eight hours a day!

It's not that retirement frightened me, but it preoccupied me nonetheless. It is one of the great changes in life, after all. I found myself haunted by the question of time; in retirement your time is both unlimited and restricted: unlimited because you are no longer constrained by the rhythm of work, but restricted because you have to face the fact that time is running out, that you do not have that eternity of life and good health in front of you, that you could believe in when you were young. So I was filled with a sense of urgency: a feeling that what I want to do must be done now and without hanging about.

As a teenager, I dreamed of setting off around the world with nothing but a pack on my back, rather like Laurie Lee's beautiful account of walking through Spain, in *As I walked out one midsummer morning*. Set out into the far blue yonder, with no more than the necessary minimum on my back, and discover the world: that's how I imagined myself in those days. Then life and its choices intervened, and in the end I stayed put, more or less: I changed countries and worked on three different continents, but it wasn't the same. Now that I had all the time in the world and nothing to hold me back, was this not the moment to realise my teenage dream? Sad indeed is the man who abandons his dreams, even if he doesn't necessarily bring them to fruition. Nonetheless, the dreams of youth have been overlaid by the accumulation of fifty extra years of life, with its joys but also its knocks and I also needed solitude and a chance to meditate. I hoped not just to discover the world, but to go in search of myself.

Life at work often locks us into an endless round, like the workings of a gigantic machine whose operation and purpose we cannot control. At work, we often only see other people as work colleagues, and as a result, we lose sight of the other in all his or her richness. Yet we are never fully ourselves except with and through our interactions with others. So setting out on a journey also means going in search of the other.

In Australia, I had heard of a path, an old aboriginal path called the Bibbulmun Trail. It starts near Perth and runs for a thousand kilometres through the bush and noble forests of *karri* and *jarrah*, to the south coast of Western Australia. As always in Australia, it's extreme walking. No wheeled vehicles are allowed, you sleep in primitive sites that only offer water, and that only if the rain has filled the reservoir; everything that enters must also leave, no waste is allowed; during the first 200km there are no towns and nowhere to buy supplies, you must carry everything with you. And Australian nature has its perils: insects, snakes, bush fires — it is strongly recommended, if you walk alone as I intend to do, to carry a radio beacon connected by satellite that can locate you if you run into serious trouble and need to call for help. The more I read about it, the more I liked it.

My son, who is an experienced walker (Chamonix-Zermatt, the GR20 in Corsica, the three mountains of Yorkshire in an absurd time, the Horseshoe in Snowdonia in the snow, and so on), was much less enthusiastic about the idea, but he had the good sense (like the good parent he is) not to oppose it head-on. "Don't you think," he opined, "that it might not be better to start with something a little less extreme? After all, it's one thing to go for a 20km walk in the forest knowing that you can rest the next day, it's quite another to do it day after day carrying a backpack, and sleeping on the ground as well". He's right, of course, I can only agree. I should train up a little.

And so St James' Way sprang to mind (funnily enough, English speakers often know the Way by its Spanish name, the Camino de Santiago). I didn't know much about it except that it's long and that it ends in Santiago de Compostela in north-western Spain. It looked as if it should suit me perfectly: France and Spain are tamed countries, food can be found everywhere, there is no problem with accommodation and the wildlife doesn't view you as a potential dinner. The Way is centuries old, and the idea of walking in the footsteps of all those pilgrims who have followed it to Compostela over the years appealed to my sense of history.

The Camino de Santiago it shall be!

Preparations

Actually, I prepared very little.

I deliberately avoided reading other people's experiences, either on the Internet or in books. Much later, once I had completed the Camino, I read the experiences of Jean-Claude Bourlès (*Le grand Chemin de Compostelle*, 1995), and Jean-Christophe Rufin (*Immortelle randonnée*, 2013) and learned a good deal from them; they made me realise just how much the Camino has changed over the last thirty years. But the danger of imbibing too much information before leaving is that you experience things not through your own perceptions but through the perspectives proposed to you by others. In life, there are experiences that you have to live yourself in order to approach them without prejudices or preconceptions, and with an untutored, even a naive eye. So I set out, without any clear ideas about what I was going to see or who I was going to meet or even exactly where the Way went. Hence I had already been walking for several weeks before I heard of the excellent *Miam-miam dodo* guide (a must for pilgrims in France). I also set off carrying a tent, convinced I was going to have to camp to avoid paying the prohibitive cost of a hotel every night.

When you walk, there are two fundamental things you must look after: your feet, which will carry you, and your back, which will carry your backpack. For the first, you need a good pair of walking shoes with good socks; personally, I prefer shoes that cover the ankle and protect it from sprains, their only disadvantage is that they are a little heavier to wear. As protection against blisters, I applied a cream (Akileïne NOK) that softens and strengthens the skin; you have to start a few weeks before leaving, and then don't hesitate to massage your feet with the cream at the end of each day to make them feel loved. Compeed dressings are found everywhere in pharmacies along the way, and are an effective treatment for blisters. For the back, you need a good backpack, and don't skimp on the price. A good backpack is lightweight, with a strong waist belt that allows you to carry the weight on the pelvis and not the shoulders, and preferably with a system to keep the bag off your back and let the air circulate. For clothes, wear synthetics that are easy to wash and that dry quickly (merino wool is more expensive but is especially good if it's likely to be cold).

If you're not already used to walking, it's a good idea to get your body into the habit. You'll train up along the Way, to be sure, but it shouldn't come as a shock. I therefore embarked on the circumnavigation of Paris by the GR1:[1] a big 650km loop through the surrounding countryside that I walked over three years, on odd days when I had the time. On the first day out, I finished after about twenty kilometres with my knees in a terrible state, especially going down a staircase where every step had me in agony. But after a hot shower and a night's sleep I found that I had recovered, so I concluded that I wasn't permanently crippled, and I did it again. A few sections of the GR later, and my legs were fine.

One day, I thought I should check for weight. So I loaded my backpack with seven 1.5-litre bottles of water (total weight, 10.5kg) and walked 36km. I came home tired but with my body still in working order, so I concluded that I was ready to leave.

During these walks, and even more so on the Way, I learned that

---

[1] A GR in France is a "chemin de grande randonnée", roughly equivalent to the National Trail system in Britain but much more extensive.

you have to listen to your body. Or rather, that you have to listen to it but only up to a point. So for example, when you get up in the morning and your body says, "We're going to walk another 25 km today? Are you out of your mind? Let's stay in bed!" you firmly invite it to shut up. But when, along the Way, you feel it say politely, "Well then, we've been walking for two hours, don't you think we should stop for a while?", then you should listen. That way, you avoid the perils of tendonitis, which puts an end to any inclination to walk for weeks or even months.

Since we're on the subject of tendonitis, don't forget to drink plenty of water, between one litre and three litres a day depending on the heat. I know that many people like to carry those backpacks that contain a pocket for water, personally I don't find them very practical. It's true that they're easy to drink from while you're walking, but then you lose the excuse to stop and take a breather. I prefer by far a bottle with a shoulder-strap, easy to access, practical to drink from, and above all practical to fill. No one will refuse you if you stop at a house and ask for water, especially not along the Way, and it's a good chance to chat and learn a little bit about the country you're passing through: to open up to others.

All that being said, there is still one crucial preparation that cannot be avoided. You must decide where to start.

The Ways are many and varied, though they all lead to Compostela. In the past, and to this day as I discovered, pilgrims came from all over Europe, from northern Germany and Flanders via Paris and Tours, from Brittany along the Atlantic coast, from Italy via Arles, from Switzerland and from southern Germany via Le Puy en Velay, which remains today the busiest of the Ways in France, and from central Germany via Vézelay.

I decided to start in Vézelay. In part, it was a tribute to my parents. They were young when they first saw the city and its basilica, and its beauty captivated them. As they got older, they returned there every year, and after my mother's death visiting Vézelay became for my father a pilgrimage in her memory.

I still remembered visiting Vézelay when I was a child. An immense luminous space of pure and sobre white stone, daring pillars that soar towards arches improbably far away in the heights of the church, where shadows play with the light. History has accumulated in this nave, I could almost feel the presence of its builders and of the countless pilgrims who had passed through it over the centuries.

Suddenly, I had to see Vézelay again, in all its calm beauty, needing no additions, self-sufficient; it would be my launching pad towards my unknown.

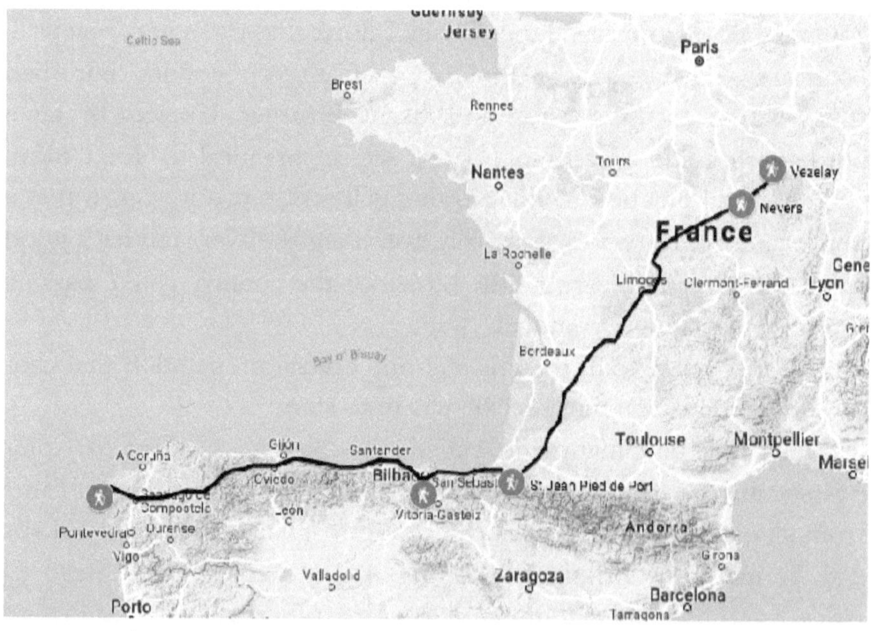

And so the Way would take me from Vézelay to Nevers, then through Limoges and Périgueux to St Jean Pied de Port. Most people then cross the Pyrenees to reach Roncesvalles in Spain and so set out on the Camino Francés, the "French Way", which passes through Burgos and León and crosses the Meseta. But I didn't like the idea of crossing that immense plain in the height of summer, so I planned instead to leave St Jean Pied de Port by the GR10 and walk to Irun on the north coast of Spain along the peaks of the Pyrenees. From Irun, I would follow the Camino del Norte along the coast, taking advantage of the cool sea breezes, to Oviedo where I intended to branch off onto the Camino Primitivo, the very first of the pilgrimage routes, and so finally to Compostela.

I planned to cut the journey in two. I was still at work in 2016, so I decided to take a short week's break for a trial run of about 100km from Vézelay to Nevers. Then in 2017, I would have retired and have all the time in the world to start again from Nevers in the hope of reaching Compostela.

2016 : from Vézelay to Nevers

So it was that in 2016, I found myself once again walking up Vézelay's main street (almost the only street in fact) that leads steeply towards the basilica on its eternal hill, as the people like to call it here. A street with houses all made of stone, old stone weathered by time that always reminds me of my childhood. My native city too is all made of stone and sometimes I used to dream of becoming a stonemason and spending my life shaping the stone with my hands and revealing in its contours the shapes of human thought.

All along the street there are shops, fashion shops, winemakers, art galleries, all rather expensive and gentrified. Many years have passed since the Vézelay of the great days of pilgrimage, when the abbey was still attached to the basilica, before its decline. The town was more turbulent then, the burghers were not yet bourgeois, riots against the feudal authority of the abbot were frequent and harshly suppressed. There were more pilgrims, they were probably poorer and certainly more fervent. More fervent than me anyway; it's many a long year since I went into a church to pray.

Entering the basilica again, though, even I could almost fall to my knees in wonder. Vézelay is undoubtedly one of the world's finest examples of Romanesque architecture. Everything is sober, peaceful, harmonious, the light fills the magnificent nave which rises boldly to the heavens. Fortunately for me, on that day there were few pilgrims, indeed few visitors of any kind, and the sensation of transcendence was complete.

10

We owe the church's extraordinary luminosity to advances in building techniques and changes in fashion. The Romanesque church was barely completed when the abbot decided to modernise it, by demolishing the choir and rebuilding it in the new Gothic style with its bigger windows and airier space.

The author Romain Rolland lived in Vézelay, and died there. The town boasts a museum dedicated to him. I admire Romain Rolland for his refusal to bow to patriotic hysteria during the 1914-18 war, for his refusal to abandon his friendship with the Austrian Stefan Zweig, and for his fidelity to his anti-militarist principles during the terrible times of 1939-45. As luck would have it, the night I arrived the company *Les Tréteaux du Monde* was putting on a single performance of Rolland's play "The Wolves", which he completed in just one week as a response to the Dreyfus affair. The plot is based on an episode during the French revolutionary wars, at the siege of Mainz. It recounts the conflict between two revolutionary commanders: Verrat, a former butcher, whose ambition is as devoid of ideas as it is of scruples; confronting him is Teulier, a member of the Académie and a fervent theoretician of Liberty. Verrat, for his own advancement, falsely accuses a rival *ci-devant*[2] officer and has him executed without trial, while Teulier denounces the injustice of the execution even at the risk of his own life. The powerful dialogue rings true. Teulier embodies revolutionary inflexibility at its most terrible and its most splendid: terrible in its readiness to sacrifice the real flesh and blood human being to an abstract belief; splendid in its conviction that it is possible to improve the fate of all humanity and so to go beyond the insignificance of the lone individual. Teulier would have appreciated the words of the Bolshevik Joffe: one can only be fully human at the service of

---

[2] An expression used to designate someone of aristocratic origins or who had otherwise benefited from the privileges of the *Ancien régime*. In this case, a military officer who had abandoned the nobility and thrown in his lot with the revolutionary cause.

something greater than oneself.

Theatre is art without a safety net and I should go more often. The troupe rose splendidly to the challenge. I returned to my hotel room to sleep not just moved, but even shaken.

I set out the next day. The weather was ideal, sunny and warm without being overwhelming. Shortly after leaving Vézelay, the Way passes by the chateau of Bazoches, once the home of the great Vauban who was Louis XIV's master of fortifications, and I paused for a moment to pay tribute to him, and to visit the little church nearby where he is buried. The castle is rather as I imagine the man. A little heavy, solidly set on its foundations, modest and without unnecessary ostentation, even a mite old-fashioned, nothing like the splendid chateau of Vaux-le-Vicomte that was built for Nicolas Fouquet, the Sun King's Minister of Finance before his disgrace (but that is another story...). Vauban first came to the notice of Cardinal Mazarin and the King for his skills as a siege engineer. Remarkably for the period, he did not seek glory and was deeply concerned for the lives of his soldiers, indeed his entire military system was designed to avoid unnecessary deaths. A contemporary described him in these words:

> *He was perhaps the most honest and virtuous man of his century, and, with the greatest reputation as the most learned in the art of sieges and fortifications, the simplest, truest and most modest... there was never a gentler, more compassionate, more obliging man... and the most miserly husbandman of men's lives, with a character that took everything upon itself, and gave everything to others.*

You can see Vauban's fortifications all over France. He even coined the French expression *"le pré carré"* (literally, a square field). In idiomatic French the expression indicates a political or even personal space to be defended, and it perfectly describes Vauban's system of fortification in Flanders. In this region in the north of France the terrain is flat, without high ground to provide natural strongholds.

Vauban invented a system of forts arranged in squares in which invading armies could be slowed down and bottled up.

Vauban's constant travels around the kingdom brought home to him the wretchedness of the peasants, whose plight was all the greater as a result of Louis XIV's incessant wars. Like all wars, these were hideously costly in both treasure and men. Horrified by the injustice of the peasants' situation, Vauban prepared a book, *La Dîme du Roy* ("The King's tithe"), in which he proposed (what a heresy!) to tax the nobility to provide for the country. The king listened politely to his proposal, but unsurprisingly it never got off the ground. One can only wonder how differently history might have turned out if it had.

. . .

I like unexpected encounters.

When you go for a Sunday walk, you choose your route: "I know, let's go to Fontainebleau forest, that's a beautiful walk". Which is not untrue, and you can enjoy a very pleasant day. Still, you know where you're going, more or less. There's not much room for the unexpected.

On the Camino, the Way chooses you. By that I mean that, once you start, you have to follow the path without knowing where it will take you, or what it will show you. Following the Camino also means, I think, keeping your heart and eyes open; otherwise, you will miss out on the unusual encounters it offers.

Look at this tree trunk, for example. It's just a tree cut down by the side of the path; it was diseased perhaps, or maybe it had suffered too much from a storm. There's nothing special about it. But take the time to look at it... Strength, abundance, time, emanates from it. Its solidity, hardness, the lines and notches left by the saw, all speak of the slow power of its growth over the years. The colour of the wood, rich as honey, evokes a nourishing soil and a full harvest in this month of September, hesitating between smouldering summer and

the softly approaching autumn. The sheer size of the trunk and —
when you look closer — the growth rings, speak to you of the passage of time. This tree may have been older than me, and it reminded
me of my grandfather who was not, to my child's eyes, unlike a tree:
his face wrinkled as if he had been hewn out of time, his movements
slow as branches in the wind, and when he walked one could well
imagine that a tree, if it could walk, would walk like that. And I remember that when my grandfather recounted his own youth, what he
had seen and experienced, it seemed to me as strange and fascinating
as if he were talking about a different planet.

I had more encounters during those first days, and not just with trees. On the first evening, at the hostel there were two friends walking the Camino together: she, a French woman in her forties from Brittany, who had already walked the Camino twice from Mont St Michel; he, a 73-year-old German, had set off once again on the Way to escape the stress of an imminent operation against cancer. They were both married, though not to each other, and they had met on the Way. Their's seemed an unusual relationship and I liked it for that very reason. We chatted together in Spanish, which turned out to be our only common language, the German spoke to me of the many times he had walked the Camino, from Barcelona, from Lisbon, from Germany. The Frenchwoman said to me: "The Camino is like life: there are wonderful parts, there are boring parts, and some parts that you would frankly rather have avoided". That seemed to me to be a very good philosophy to face the Way and life: nothing lasts forever, even the most difficult times.

Another meeting, this time with a Dutch computer scientist, preoccupied with the implications of Artificial Intelligence: how will moral decisions be integrated into AI algorithms? How will a stand-alone car behave if a child runs in front of it, and its AI has to choose between running down the child or crashing into a wall and killing its occupant? It's a difficult question indeed, and I had no idea of the answer, indeed I confess I had never even thought about it. But the discussion, until late at night, opened up perspectives and questions that I would not have thought of. My only regret, when I woke up the next morning, was the awareness that I could only remember fragments of our conversation; I resolved to keep a notebook by me to jot down ideas that arise as discussions and days go by.

The following day, I came across another Dutch IT engineer, a DBA (Database administrator) this time. He was a living expression of the way our profession can shape our view of the world, and confided in me a project he dreamed of undertaking: collecting recorded interviews in which people recount their lives, their experiences, their dreams.

"What people?", I asked.

"Why, everybody!", he replied.

A database of dreams! What a beautiful idea! I'm well aware that it's perfectly unrealistic, but what a fine ambition all the same! My Dutch acquaintance seemed so surprised to find someone who took his dream seriously, and was even enthusiastic about it, that we ended up talking half the evening. The next morning, I woke up early (practically inevitable when you sleep in a tent). Opening the tent flap, I found an anonymous gift placed on the ground: a little knife, a few coins, and a note. It could only have come from my collector of dreams, and I wondered whether I should wait to speak to him. But then, he wanted to remain anonymous and it seemed to me that I should respect that, so I left silently and went on my way into a cool and sunlit Burgundian morning.

I came at last to Nevers, the year's final destination. For the first time I realised how discouraging it can be for a walker to come to a large town. You see the signpost announcing the city boundary and you think you've arrived, but of course you haven't (I should have thought of this before): you still have several kilometres to go before the city centre. An hour or two's walking, on tarmac which is hard on the feet, and your eyes locked down by the seemingly endless straight lines of streets, pavements, houses, apartment blocks, or distracted by the street furniture full of signs but without significance. And then, I don't much go for the houses in the suburbs. It's true that now and then you come across an unexpectedly whimsical garden, but on the whole they leave you with the feeling that each house, far from expressing its inhabitants' individuality, is merely another number in an endless vista of the commonplace. You have to get to the city centre as soon as possible, where people are piled up together and there are bars, and restaurants, and shops, and all the places where people can meet. There, there is life. But not in Nevers, at least not today. I arrived there at the beginning of a Friday afternoon, there wasn't a soul in the streets and even the great flat space of the Parc Roger Salengro was empty. There was nothing for me there, and I made a beeline for the station and the train that would take me back to Paris.

A few days later, I went back to the Camino in my mind's eye. I realised that new ideas had made an appearance in my mind, or perhaps rather they were ideas already present but rearranged so that they became clearer. How could that happen but without my being aware of it?

I had a vague memory of a particularly gruelling day. The Camino ran for the most part along the road, between fields. It was 35° in the shade, except there was no shade: nothing but wheat as far as the eye could see. During the last 15km my mind switched off, my surroundings receded till all that remained was the slow progress of one foot following another. I had the feeling that I had reached the state of non-consciousness which Zen monks call the antechamber of wisdom. This had always left me sceptical in the past, and yet there's no getting away from the experience: reducing the conscious mind to silence for a while allowed the unconscious to rise to the surface, giving it time to sort out ideas, to examine them from different angles, and finally to present them to the conscious mind in a different light. This unconscious activity is one of the functions of dreams during sleep, "chief nourisher of life's feast" as Macbeth said, but they had never left me with such a feeling of clarity. Perhaps there is something different about this sleeping state which is not really sleep, because the conscious mind remains present and able to dialogue with the unconscious?

At all events, something seemed to have changed in me. I had met new people, and I had walked alone, and I had found that both offered me more than I had dared to expect. And I realised that

where before the Camino was ethereal, a dream, it had become concrete, a need.

18

In via in patria

On my return home, I recounted to Florence my experiences on the Way, and its effect on me. I confided to her my intention to write an account of my journey, my ambition to set my pen to something more personal than the technical reports that I had spent so much of my working life writing. I shared with her also, my perplexity at the reasons for this ambition: why should one want to write, especially why write anything other than letters, why aim at a broader public when one probably has no particular talent for it? Shortly before my departure on the next stage of my journey, she wrote to me. Her words touched me, and accompanied me along the Way, and so I have included them here.

"My dear Martin", she began, "You are not yet on your Way but I have already left, thanks to your pilgrim's tale. I will stay here in the capital, while your footsteps will trace their path along the Way, so yes, reading your words I have already set out, for you know that words can often make us travel as far as the body's displacement in physical space.

Tell me, what is a travel log? Why write? What will you write about? The countryside you pass through, the people you meet, the difficulties you encounter? Will you talk of yourself a little, perhaps a lot... will each step, each word, not be part of that meeting with the other that you hope for and expect?

There's a bit of all that already in your description of the walk from Vézelay to Nevers. Will you continue in this literary path, will you be able to, given the fatigue of the journey? You will have to be able to walk, look, listen, meet and exchange... you will have to take the time to live in the moment. And writing is a solitary thing, it forces you to put some distance between yourself and the immediate. Do you really want to place that distance between yourself and the moment as you live it, aren't you afraid to corrupt the moment by intellectualising it through writing?

You didn't write between Vézelay and Nevers, you only undertook that 'labour' on your return, going back over your memories and impressions, leaving your memory the time to recompose what you had lived through. Some things you forgot of course, but forgetfulness can be useful because it leaves behind only what is essential, what the experience has left in you. What you forgot, probably you forgot because the memory was not important enough for you.

I wanted to dedicate to you St Augustine's magnificent expression: '*In via in patria*'. Did you know that long before we met, I had pinned these words to the wall in my office at work, as a sort of challenge to the sedentary life I am forced to live, even though I know very well that Augustine was speaking metaphorically.

Our country is the road. To live is to travel. We are at home in movement itself, it both creates and destroys what distances us from ourselves and from others. Life is movement. *In via in patria*. St Augustine is a sort of private joke for us.

You left for Vézelay, and I stayed behind. Vézelay is a mystery, a secret. Many people encouraged me to visit Vézelay but I could never understand what they expected me to find there. When at last I did go, I listened to the mineral silence of the stones, sublimated in the basilica's clear and silent space.

Vézelay was a decisive step for me. I stayed three days at the Monastery of La Pierre qui Vire, sharing the monks' morning study, the silence of their meals, and the repetition of their services: vigils, matins, evensong, compline...

Another way of living time. Another way of sharing.

I wasn't looking for God, I wanted to live with these men who have made their lives a consecration somewhere between materiality and spirituality, who produce with their hands and work the land to feed their community and yet who still, despite everything, leave time for study and the spirit, and where every day has its rightful place. A monastery is an enclave, it can receive pilgrims but the monks do not travel, or only very little, they remain where they are, always present, caring for the life and stability of this special place.

Leave or Remain. You, Martin, will be the one to leave and I will remain behind. Reading your words I discover you as you are, bursting with ideas, thoughts, longing and reflection. '*Redi in te ipsum*'. St Augustine again. 'Return to yourself'. This exhortation was addressed to himself, in his *Confessions*, his remarkable, and remarkably modern, work of introspection. Did he write to understand himself, or to bear witness? Both, no doubt.

Why write? For us, at least, it will spring from the urge to share. May the Way live in our eyes and our thoughts".

Why write indeed? Perhaps it was Nicolas Bouvier in *Le vide et le plein* who found the words that I could not:

> *The traveller writes to measure the distance that remains unknown, that he has yet to travel.*

2017: Nevers and beyond

The year after my return, I went back on the Way again. Logically enough, I started where I had left off, in Nevers.

Alighting from the train I was gripped by a vague feeling of unease. I had been thinking about this journey for so long. I wouldn't say exactly that I had planned it, rather I had prepared myself for the idea that I would undertake it. But finding myself standing there, on the station platform in Nevers with 1700km on foot ahead of me, the whole idea suddenly seemed insane. Especially the backpack, which seemed much heavier than when I set out from Vézelay; back then, after a few kilometres I hardly seemed to feel it any more. Certainly, the pack had a few more bits and pieces in it this time, the iPad especially since I planned to write along the Way (and after all, paper is heavy too); that was partly the object of the journey. Nonetheless, feeling it on my shoulders I couldn't help but wonder: "Will I really be able to keep up the pace with this pack on my back? And what on earth did I put in it?".

Perhaps just putting one foot down in front of the other would be enough...

I walked up from the station towards the Espace Sainte Bernadette, an establishment run by the Holy Sisters of Charity of Nevers, where I had arranged to stay for the night. I filled in a form which proposed a broad choice of honourifics: not just the usual "Mr" and

"Mrs", but also "Father", "Monsignor", and others which I didn't even recognise. I was welcomed amiably into an edifice which seemed huge and empty, despite the activity whose noise I could vaguely hear coming from somewhere else in the building.

The Espace seemed to be made up of long, very wide, corridors, stretching off in all directions. Judging by the keys in the locks on the doors (they hadn't got round to using those electronic pass keys handed out at reception), and by the silence surrounding me, I must have been the only pilgrim in the place that night. A strange feeling of solitude came over me, being a Parisian I'm unused to being so alone, not lost in nature but in a hall of lodging where everything seemed vast, empty, and given over to contemplation. The feeling of emptiness and solitude was reinforced by the presence of two women meditating alone in a little sanctuary dedicated to St Bernadette Soubirous which could easily have held two hundred.

The only noise came from a little flock of priests I could hear talking below my window (perhaps the "young priests from Burgundy" announced by a poster in the entrance). Like a bunch of adolescents they talked, laughed, and chatted on their mobiles. But they were priests so all dressed in black, making them look like a gathering of frolicsome crows.

The outdated (but impeccably clean) decor appealed to me, reminding me of childhood holidays in France, in strange hotels similarly decorated, with the same washbasins. The only thing missing in my room was the bidet, which puzzled me considerably as a child. What on earth could they be for? I finally concluded that they must be designed for washing the feet and I found them vey practical, though I never worked out the purpose of the little fountain in the middle.

Nevers had not made a good impression on me during my previous visit, no offence to its inhabitants and their Tourist Office. I found everything heavy, especially the architecture, great heavy constructions in every tone of grey and white, devoid of delicacy, oozing bourgeois provinciality and its oppressive catholicism. But then perhaps I had been too tired to be fair, perhaps I hadn't seen the town at its best. I decided to go for a stroll, to give the town a chance to correct my first negative impression. And besides, it was all the fault of my brother, who had told me before my first visit: "The great thing about Nevers is the fast train back to Paris".

Nevers does have a fine and rather unusual cathedral. There is no great doorway opposite the altar, you can only enter the cathedral from the side. Once inside, there appear to be two altars: an ordinary one in the East as one would expect, with modern stained glass that frankly I could have done without, and then in the West... "Christ in Glory, 12ᵗʰ century" according to the little explanatory panel. But I know the Christ Pantocrator when I see him. What could he be doing here? He could be the twin brother of the mosaic images of Christ in Hagia Sophia in Istanbul, or in Ravenna, or in the Norman churches of Sicily. And this Christ, in general, is a political statement as much as an object of devotion. He is represented, not as the suffering figure on the cross but in the manner of a Byzantine emperor, in all his glory, reigning in majesty over the universe. In Sicily, this statement was combined with a declaration of independence from the Pope: in the Martorana church in Palermo, King Roger II is shown being crowned not by the Pope but directly by Christ.

To tell the truth, I think it is this Christ that made the biggest impression on me in Nevers — the Christ and the feeling of living in a bygone age in the Espace Sainte Bernadette. But the town itself did not really seem much more attractive than the first time, especially once I crossed over the Loire on an admittedly splendid bridge. What on Earth were they thinking of in the town hall when they gave planning permission, on such a magnificent site, for those two monstrous concrete blockhouses on the river bank? What on Earth are they for? I have no idea, nor do I give a jot. And so I went back to my room in the Espace, and went to bed early, to prepare myself for the following day's ordeal...

. . .

In the end, it wasn't too bad. My backpack weighed less than the day before (I wasn't so tired!), and little by little I swung into the rhythm of a solitary day's walking by the banks of the Loire and through the forests of Apremont and Grossouvre. I barely passed a living soul, unsurprisingly since I cheated on the officially marked GR which seemed obsessed with having me walk along the roads; I had suffered enough the previous year from the tarmac, so hard on my poor feet who need looking after with 1700km ahead of them. And so I branched off along side tracks through the woods, ignoring all the signs marked "Private Property".

They reminded me of an episode in that great classic of British humour, *Three men in a boat (to say nothing of the dog)* by Jerome K Jerome. It tells the tale of three young men in late 19th century London who decide to take a holiday by rowing up the Thames, camping along the way. They encounter notices of a similar kind to mine, and the author gives vent to his feelings:

> *The sight of those notice-boards rouses every evil instinct in my nature. I feel I want to tear each one down, and hammer it over the head of the man who put it up, until I have killed him, and then I would bury him, and put the board up over the grave as a tombstone.*
>
> *I mentioned these feelings of mine to Harris, and he said he had them worse than that. He said he not only felt he wanted to kill the man who caused the board to be put up, but that he should like to slaughter the whole of his family and all his friends and relations, and then burn down his house. This seemed to me to be going too far, and I said so to Harris; but he answered:*

Jerome was no doubt right to spare the family and friends but I confess that I tend instinctively to react like Harris when confronted with
these insolent affirmations of the absolute rights of Holy Private
Property. But this time, I left the signs unharmed (too high to reach!),
and merely ignored them as I walked into the woods. Thinking about
it later, I even pardoned the proprietors who almost certainly could
not have opened access to their forest even had they wished to,
without inviting all sorts of problems of insurance coverage and
such-like insanities. Or perhaps it was just the same kind of ban as
the one on fishing in the lake of the park where I live, in the Paris
suburbs. The sign says "No fishing", but this doesn't stop Sunday
fishermen from turning up, loaded down with expensive and sophisticated fishing tackle, to see if they can land a carp; and when they
catch a big one, they call the Town Hall to have it weighed and pho-
tographed, with them alongside it.

Whatever. I took my chances and walked on through the woods,
though not without a passing thought, that I would be in a real fix
were I to fall and break a leg in this isolated forest, where visibly
nobody ever came, and without reception for my mobile to boot.

After Grossouvre came the Berry canal. At first I couldn't see it
anywhere, although according to the map I should have been walking
alongside it. Then I realised that the half-buried trench beside the

path was the canal. The Berry canal is no longer in use, and for the first few kilometres it is not even supplied with water.

I am always saddened by an abandoned canal, or an abandoned railway line. When they were built, they were masterpieces of civil engineering, hacked out by main force from the living body of the Earth. To this day, a labourer is called a "navvy" in spoken English, that is to say a "navigator". In the 18th and 19th centuries they criss-crossed the country in great disorderly and almost uncontrollable bands, with their women and children, living like outlaws, or rather, outside the law, especially the law of the Church. They took no care for their immortal souls, much to the displeasure of the respectable. They were the beginnings of a modern proletariat, freeing itself little by little from the norms of feudal society and standing up against its oppressors. Every time I see their abandoned works, no longer used, I think of them, heroes despite themselves, who laboured so hard, and it seems to me a terrible waste.[3]

---

[3] To relive their experience in song, you can't do better than listen to "Poor Paddy works on the railway", interpreted by the Pogues.

Farewell to the Berry canal

As I began to think about writing up the next stage of the journey, I reread Nicolas Bouvier's wonderful book *The way of the world*. I suddenly realised how absurd it was, to have wanted to take him as a model. Quite apart from the fact that I don't begin to have his talent, I'm trying to do something very different. Bouvier wrote (or at least, published) *The way of the world* ten years after his journey, in the early 1950s, from Switzerland to India. He must have spent ten years thinking about it, going back over his notes and memories, talking it over perhaps with his friend Thierry Viernet with whom he travelled, all that in the interstices of life when he wasn't earning his keep, falling in love, bringing up children, and all the rest that makes life... life.

What I want to aim for is a sort of instantaneous writing: to bring together reflections, impressions, encounters along the way, and to give them form if not the same day, then at least at no more than a few days' interval. Perhaps to overcome the danger that Florence pointed out to me, of corrupting the immediate through writing; perhaps rather, to try to capture the immediate in writing. I've never tried to do this before... but then I've never tried to walk the Camino before either, so both can be seen as experimental.

I'm reminded suddenly of my friend the poet (who certainly never made any money from his poetry). Amongst other pieces, he wrote what you might call the poem of his life. How long did it take him? Oh, forty years spent writing before he finally published it in a tiny booklet, at his own expense. He distributes it, with an almost embarrassed air, to select friends; he may even have sold a few copies. One thing is certain, he never bothered about how many "likes" he got. Not, you understand, that one can't take any pleasure at the idea that what you write is appreciated, quite the contrary. But the first measure of success must be the rightness and honesty of the writing, at least so it seems to me. And of course, you try to make it interesting.

Back to the Berry canal... I ended up following it all the way from Grossouvre to St Amond Montrond. I really saw no reason why I should leave the canal to wander about in the hills as the GR on the map proposed I should. And I understood at last the difference between a walker and a pilgrim. The walker may decide on his route, but has no destination: the walk is an activity sufficient unto itself. But the pilgrim has a destination, or rather he has two: the physical goal of the pilgrimage (Compostela in my case), and then his Grail, so to speak: what he is looking for, perhaps without even being aware of it, so that the pilgrimage is undertaken both in the world and within himself. Since he has a destination, the pilgrim avoids detours: certainly, he wants to see the country he walks through, but he is not walking to admire the view. So the Way leaves the GR to its picturesque meanderings and forges straight ahead (relatively speaking of course, since it avoids major roads where the traffic is dangerous, disagreeable, and destructive of meditation, and makes an effort to avoid that mortal enemy of the walker: tarmac). The canal is thus perfectly suited to the pilgrim's state of mind.

The canal has a hypnotic effect, I found. Kilometre after kilometre, it goes on dead straight, broken only by an occasional bridge, and at intervals of one kilometre more or less, a lock. At each lock there is the same little house, where the lock-keeper used to live, with the distances marked on it, to St Amond in one direction and to Bourges in the other. This gave me an idea of the physical reality of a kilometre: it corresponds roughly to the maximum distance at which

I can distinguish objects. Looking ahead, somewhere in the direction of infinity, infinitely small and infinitely far away, I could make out a little white house by the canal... that's one kilometre, and there are another twenty-five to go. I remembered my friend the poet again, who — when I spoke to him of my proposal to walk the Way — told me of his military service, when he had to do forced marches of 200km in three days, with 30kg on the back plus the "light infantry weapon" (which became less and less so, as the day wore on), and the obligation to help out the less resistant squaddies.

"We were young, we were handsome, and we were dumb", as he said, and to top it all he was really unsuited to military discipline (he still is, even more so if possible), and found himself often enough in a punishment platoon. Today we are neither so young nor so handsome. There's nothing to be done about it, but whether we remain as dumb is entirely up to us: another reason to go on pilgrimage.

That said, I couldn't help wondering, as I considered my own much smaller backpack, how he had been able to carry his 30kg, or how indeed such a thing could be humanly possible. In my time I have had to lift 50kg sacks of cement, which really tried the limits of my strength, before these were replaced by 25kg sacks (which were a relief, but heavy enough nonetheless), and I couldn't help thinking that I would have been one of the less resistant squaddies. Luckily for me there is no military service in Britain.

Since we're talking about my backpack, well, I began to feel that I really should have weighed it before setting out. I had no idea how much it weighed, all I knew is that it was too much, and that the pack kept reminding me of its presence more often than was frankly agreeable. There was nothing useless in it, I was sure, but was everything in it strictly necessary? For a moment I wondered whether this would be a good proverb for life itself, but then threw the idea aside: to live life without anything useless would be a dismal and utilitarian philosophy, and then, how do you define the useless anyway?

Are art, friendship, those things which serve only to give pleasure to yourself and others to be classed as "useless"? If life had to be useful, what would be the use of life?

Florence's words shortly before my departure came back to me: a "walker before the Eternal", she called me. In a sense it's true, though I'm no kind of believer in an eternal God. But I had to confess that in the immediate, the Eternal seemed very far off, the sense of my sins weighed a good deal less than the pack on my back, Jerusalem seemed somewhat closer than the next village, and the salvation of my immortal soul preoccupied me considerably less than the suspicion of a blister forming on my foot. Notwithstanding, now and then, the Eternal appeared to me crossing a field full of flowers, or when a ray of sunlight pierced the canopy of trees as the Way wended through a wood.

But then, what exactly is this Eternal anyway?

Perhaps, behind every mystic experience lies what Freud called the "oceanic feeling", the sensation of being one with nature and the universe, the universe being the closest that a human being can imagine as "eternal". I think this must be as old as humankind itself, even that it is a permanent facet of the human condition.

If you look at the beliefs of all the archaic peoples, they always seem to have three major preoccupations.

The first is a feeling of alienation from nature. In their creation legends, we always find the idea that at the beginning of time, human beings, animals and spirits were not separate from one another, and had not taken on a definitive form. Animals could take on human form and vice versa. But in our days this is no longer the case and only the shamans can cross the threshold that separates humans from the animal or spirit worlds. This is the price we pay for self-consciousness, the awareness of ourselves as individuals, different from other humans and separate from nature, which is — to use Marx's fine expression — our "natural body". It is a necessary and even an inevitable price to pay, but a price nonetheless. It is like our awareness of our separation from our mother at birth, and surely it is not for nothing that nature, the Earth, appears so often in ancient myths in the female form of the "nourishing Earth". One should go on from there to think more deeply about humanity's relationship to nature, about what it has been in the past and about what it could, and should, be... but that goes way beyond my limited ambitions here.

Since we must live with this awareness of separation, we must also live with the awareness of death. It seems that it took a very long time for the idea to emerge that death could draw a definitive line under an individual's existence. That said, the soul's destiny after death was seen very differently in different cultures. For many, the soul remains as a mere shadow of the living individual in flesh and blood. Is the soul malignant or benign? There too, cultures differ, though one common feature is an invocation of the deceased, that they should depart in peace and not remain to trouble the living.

And finally, there is the question of the "why" behind it all. Why does the world exist? Why do we exist? How did it, and we, come into existence? And was there anything before? In the question of the "how?", and in the attempts to influence events in the real world through magic, we can see the ancestors of scientific thought.

One question that came to me as I walked, especially in those moments when the pack really weighed me down, was the idea of approaching the Eternal though "the mortification of the flesh". In Christianity the physical body (especially, of course, the female body) is often treated as something unclean, obscure, a source of sin and I find that idea frankly unhealthy, morbid even. It is common enough, on the other hand, to encounter practices which put the body "in difficulty" with the aim of gaining knowledge beyond the conscious mind. In North America, for example, many of the first peoples would practice fasting, until the spirits spoke to them in dreams or visions; in India, holy men still use breathing exercises to slow the metabolism, with the same aim.

To return to my backpack then, it is certainly sent from God as an instrument for the mortification of my flesh. In the town of La Châtre I renounced my chances of sainthood by going to the Post Office and lightening my load by 2.6kg, which I sent home in a parcel. I kept telling myself that I had really been rash and badly organised to set out with so much stuff, but then in the hostel at Crozant I met someone still more so than myself, and another proof that the Way is full of odd personalities. He was a man of about my age, a very tall man, indeed a veritable tree of a man, stuck in Crozant with a foot wound got when falling in the woods, and delighted to have somebody to talk to. He told me that in his youth he had been a painter, and that after completing his military service he had joined the French Foreign Legion to see something of the world. Like my friend the poet, he too had stories of forced marches with a heavy load. But when the time came for him to set off on the Way, he took no account of the passage of time and merrily left home with 30kg on his back, as if he were still in his twenties. He wanted to be completely autonomous — I could sympathise with that, but I had very quickly understood how unrealistic it was — and so he set off with everything but the kitchen sink on his back. He also wanted to be autonomous with regard to maps, so the first day out from Vézelay he got lost in the middle of nowhere and someone had to come and rescue him; the second day, he well and truly sprained his ankle, and carried on walking nonetheless. Since then, it had to be said, he had gained a certain sense of reality and lightened his load... but only by 5kg, which meant that he was still carrying double the weight that I find rather too heavy (please accept my apologies, gentle reader, if you find all these reflections on backpacks and kilograms tedious; take the Way some day, and you will see how obsessional about them one can become). An artist-painter who defines himself as such is unusual, but one who has volunteered for the Legion is positively rare, and I was curious. He explained that he had indeed earned his keep as a painter, but more as a ceramist specialising not just in ceramic objects but more particularly in monuments and restorations. He might be called in, for example, by a church whose stained glass had been lost, or hidden by a later building, to create a ceramic replacement which would give an idea of the original. There was a great deal of historical research involved, he told me, and a great deal of thought; I could well believe him. And I found we agreed that one could really do without the modern stained glass in the cathedral at Nevers.

But how did he end up in the Legion? Ah the Legion, he said, you have to understand that it's a great family of misfits and people who want to see the world. He had met, in the Legion, a Swiss pilot who had deserted, with his fighter, to France, and then any number of anti-militarist anarchist refugees from the student movements of 1968... a bizarre world indeed, full of unexpected destinies.

...

To go back to the Berry canal, since we were on the subject, two things in particular struck me as I walked.

The first was how much the countryside made me think of my childhood in Oxford and the Cotswolds — a sensation which remained undiminished after leaving the canal and even after leaving the Berry for the Indre. There are the same little fields and hedgerows surrounded by vast fields of wheat, the same gentle, undulating countryside, the same colours with that rich green of the trees standing out so clearly on the deep blue background of the sky, the same enormous, noble trees, the same climate (the French like to say that it rains all the time in England, but all this greenery in the Berry can't grow without rain, as I found out). Nonetheless, there is one great difference: Oxford is only 80km from London, while the Berry is miles from anywhere. By "anywhere" of course, I mean Paris, Lyon, and Toulouse, the three major industrial and commercial centres of France. Even the locals say so: one was to tell me later that the Berry is a region where nothing ever entered, and nothing ever left, and where the railways closed down almost as soon as they opened. Oxford, half way between London and Birmingham on the M40 motorway, is no longer properly speaking at the heart of a rural region: rather, the town is a component of an industrial and financial centre which extends West from London to the IT industries along the M4 Corridor and North as far as Birmingham. Which means, that you never find around Oxford the half-deserted villages so characteristic of French rural desertification; on the contrary, there is nary a cottage, however dilapidated, that has not been lovingly restored and whose owner works, not in the countryside but in an office in London, Maidenhead, Reading, or Oxford itself.

The second thing that struck me was the contrast between the industrial and the agricultural Berry. All along the canal, I came across the marks of industrial activity, from a tile factory in Grossouvre, still in operation, to St Amond, which I'll come back to. But as soon as I left the canal, I plunged into the heart of rural France: the land is rich, the soil a deep brown that bespeaks its fertility, the Charolais cattle are healthy and well fed; in one field, I even spotted an enormous bull in the middle of the herd. Thanks to the cattle, in this month of May there were also hay fields full of flowers, unlike the wheat fields which have been emptied of any other vegetation by pesticides. You can see the difference in the houses too. The workers' houses, usually just a single storey, do not cut so fine a figure as the richer houses in the villages.

Sadness of a working man and the countryside

Walking along the canal was mostly a solitary business, but from time to time I did encounter another human being. In the vagueness of the morning as the fallen rain rose in mist from the thick grass of the path, I made out something moving far away down the towpath. For a long time I could make out nothing but a form, or sometimes two forms, engaged in some strange dance; I couldn't even determine if they were coming towards me, in which case our paths might eventually cross, or heading away from me into a permanent state of mysteriousness. What could these forms be? Sometimes they seemed to be a man and a bicycle which the rider would alternately mount and dismount, then the bicycle would seem to disappear altogether. They more I walked the more I stared ahead, and the more perplexed I became until at last the distance between us closed enough for me to determine that the mysterious figures were indeed coming in my direction, and then, some time later, to put to rest the slightly unnerving prospect of an animated bicycle, as the smaller of the two figures resolved itself into a dog frolicking around its master. What could be more ordinary, in short, especially in the countryside, than a man out walking his dog? Nonetheless, he did seem to be behaving strangely. I could just see that he carried a stick with which he regularly brushed the long grass alongside the path, not in the desultory fashion of a walker idly sweeping the raindrops off the grass into the morning light, but with a definite air of purpose. My mystery seemed to have resolved itself into another mystery. At last — and this whole business must have caused me a good three quarters of an hour of perplexity — we passed each other on the towpath and I could see that he was carrying a large sack half full of snails. Here, of course, was the mystery's answer: the previous night's rain had brought out the snails in quantity: great big round, beautiful Burgundy snails, obviously destined for culinary oblivion. I was tempted to pause and make conversation, but the solitary snail man seemed singularly uncommunicative and we went on our respective ways.

The fishermen on the other hand, clearly out for a day's uninterrupted peace and solitude along the canal, with a catch a bonus rather than an objective, were more loquacious, greeting me as I passed with a few friendly words; they were invariably accompanied by dogs which seemed as amiable as their owners.

The last of these, encountered just before I reached St Amond, had finished his day and was happy to chat. I learned that in the canal, they fished for pike and zander (no, I had never heard of it either), that some would simply return their catch to the canal while others would eat them, and that a fine pike was considered a delicacy, to be served around Christmas or New Year.

My new acquaintance turned out to be another recent retiree, and glad of it. I learnt that he had been a worker in the jewellery industry, and that St Amond had once been well known for its production of jewellery and gold medallions; back in the day, there had been sixteen different companies with their workshops in the town. All that is finished now, the workshops have closed down and only two companies are left, doing no more than repairs and refurbishment. He had taken the offer of early retirement when the new owner of his company had decided to stop production of medallions in France rather than replace the stamping press, which was no longer up to modern standards. And he added, "The boss wanted to send me out to Thailand, to set the press up for the little Chinks" (he used the word without any animosity), "but I didn't want to. What was I going to do out there?".

What to make of this? To me it seemed the chance of a lifetime: to leave St Amond for a journey to the other end of the world, to meet other people there, and better still to work with them — but my jeweller acquaintance wanted nothing to do with it, preferring to fish in peace along the canal and to show off an impressive photo of the pike he had caught the previous Christmas.

I was to encounter this sadness of the rural world and its small-scale industry over and over again.

One evening when I had been unable to find a place to stay, and was on the point of bivouacking in front of the local church (after all, if a pilgrim can't set up his tent by the church...), a charming couple welcomed me with much grace into their home; he had been a farmer, a massive man with a disarming, gentle smile, who shook hands with one of the biggest palms I have ever seen, while she had worked in the legal system. I asked them how people got along in the region, since agriculture seemed to offer a living to fewer and fewer people. The farmer explained how much agriculture had changed: he had farmed 72ha with twenty cattle, by himself, but today there are no farms smaller than 200ha. The young farmers (this said with a sad shake of the head) try organic farming, or goats, but they work alone and slave away from dawn to dusk, it's no way to live.

His wife, to my astonishment, replied: the psychiatric hospitals. She could name three in the area, but then there were also the psychiatric outpatients placed in host families — apparently it pays well.

All of a sudden I remembered a B&B on my second night out from Nevers. Not at all my usual kind of place: too dear for my budget, too fussily decorated for my taste (but very comfortable, and the food was irreproachable). My hostess showed me the various craft products that she sold to her guests, amongst which I saw a soap made with asses' milk. I could hardly believe my eyes: just like Cleopatra! Obviously, it was very expensive; a local farmer kept twenty donkeys solely to provide milk for soap. Who could afford such things, I wondered? Surely only city-dwellers sufficiently well-off to afford luxury holidays (my B&B even had stabling for horses), accompanied by local produce, *"du terroir"* as they say in France. And it occurred to me that the whole rural economy has been turned upside down. The countryside is not only losing its population, it has become completely dependent on the cities. Once the towns depended on the countryside to feed them, while the countryside, at a pinch, could feed itself. Today, the countryside is completely dependent on the cities which supply the increasingly sophisticated machinery on which farming depends, but also the market for its production. Farm products could never find sufficient markets in the surrounding countryside, even the most extravagant feudal lord would not know what to do with it all. And the "local produce" is very different from what it once was, when I came to France as a child; today it is the luxury or semi-luxury produce of a sort of sub-economy which exists in a parasitic relationship with the international economy and large-scale industry.

Further along the Way, in the agreeable little town of Cluis, I dropped in to the Luma Bar for my morning coffee. The bar seemed much too cosy to be French, and indeed it turned out to be run by an English couple... I beg your pardon, I'm committing the usual French blunder... by a Welsh couple (drop in yourselves, it's worth a look and they brew their own beer).

Hannah, who looks after the bar, served me a good strong coffee and I asked her about local life. She spoke of the hidden poverty, that nobody talks about and that remains out of sight, the inevitable result of high unemployment; and of those who have not worked for so long that they no longer know how, and who eke out a minimal existence barely sustained by the RSA (social security benefit).

To my surprise, she also spoke of the local English poor. She knew about twenty such people, who thought they had hit the jackpot when even a working-class house in Britain could be sold for a substantial sum, following the explosion of house prices as a result of the frenetic speculation under first the Thatcher government, then those that followed during the 1990s. Arriving in France they were able to buy and renovate charming houses in the countryside. But the jackpot melted away over the years, and they found themselves having to make do on very little, even less since Brexit has led to a 25% drop in the value of sterling.

Still further on, in the little town of Bénévent l'Abbaye, I had the pleasure of exercising my mother tongue in the company of an English engineer who had a small specialised building business there. "Here", he said, "when someone goes for a job interview, money is never mentioned. Everybody simply assumes that the job pays the minimum wage".

He told me of a 180ha farm nearby where he had recently done some levelling work. It still had a fine manor house and even stables for twenty horses, and one could imagine how many people would have been needed just to look after the house and the horses, let alone to work the farm. But today, the farm belongs to a Danish company which has taken on a single Danish manager, who farms 180ha of cereal by himself, with a single tractor and its assorted attachments. In the near future, it is quite possible that one person will be able to manage several farms using robotic tractors guided by GPS, without ever leaving Copenhagen.

So much sadness, so many lives hemmed in and restricted by an economy that cares not a jot about human lives, nor about the essential relationship between mankind and nature, and whose logical conclusion will be the transformation of rural France into a few entirely robotised factory farms where a human presence will be treated as a pest more than anything else.

How should I conclude these rather gloomy reflections? Perhaps by one of those flashes of hope that humanity can sometimes offer.

One night I camped on the edge of a small town that exuded that air of abandonment so common in the region, and went to eat in a shabby but welcoming pizzeria. The customers were all locals, and the manager's young daughter took delight in demonstrating her skills in dance and gymnastics to everybody who entered. As I watched her, touched and inspired by her unselfconscious enthusiasm and joy in life, a grim-faced elderly biker came in, kitted out in all the Hell's Angels gear. He evidently knew the child, and bent down to embrace her with a gesture of such tenderness that it transformed him entirely. And then he talked to her, about his great ambition, a tour of the United States to visit all the emblematic sites of the classic Westerns. I saw a man aged and knocked about by life, but whose dreams were still vibrant.

Then, as I walked down towards La Souterraine, I came across a haven of peace. Somebody had created a little enclosure in the wood that bordered the Way, for the comfort of passing pilgrims. A few large logs had been put in a circle to serve as seats, and attached to a tree was a box with the cockleshell symbol containing tobacco, and a notebook and pencil to leave a message. And I gave thanks to the person who showed me thus that the Holy Spirit of Private Property does not yet reign completely supreme.

Ascension

I received another mail from Florence that gave me much to think over, as one kilometre gave way to another.

"My dear Martin", she wrote, "this weekend is the Ascension holiday and those two verbs 'to go / to stay' with which we began our correspondence have become THE question for the Parisians! To go or to stay? The weather forecast predicts almost a heatwave for the next four days, with bright sunshine and temperatures to send you jumping straight into any water you can find.

Any Parisians who can have doubtless resigned themselves to being stuck in the traffic jams on the motorways leading out of the Capital, in search of a patch of countryside or beach, a brief moment of contact with nature. They'll be happy enough for a few days in Brittany or Normandy, at St Malo or Mont St Michel, avoiding the thought of the return journey which looks like being as hot as hell if the car has no air conditioning.

And then there are the others, who can't leave. Or who don't want to.

They stick it out, sweating in the heavy, stifling, polluted heat of the city... in a capital too full of people but astonishingly radiant with its cafés spilling into the streets where life overflows like a wave of joy, an explosion of summer exuberance.

I went walking in my district, the 11th Arrondissement, and I saw the crowded streets around Bastille through your eyes, as you walk peacefully through the Creuse. How different from your solitude!

In the heat of the day I received your SMS, telling me that you were resting from the sun, lying under a tree and listening to the birds. The Parisians were taking their coffee break.

Like you, I went looking for some shade. I went up Rue de la Roquette till I reached Place de la Bastille, feeling like holidays with my sunglasses, wearing a skirt and the back bare. I accompanied you on the Way by going on my way, on the lookout for my Paris that I know so well and want to transmit to you.

It's the holiday of Ascension. Apart from the ever fewer Christians, who in our secular society still knows what Ascension represents?

It never ceases to amaze me that we have kept such fundamentally Christian holy days as Ascension and Pentecost, just before the celebration of the French Revolution on the 14th July, a secular holiday if ever there was one.

Ascension. Or rather, taking flight. I look upwards, and there on top of its column and framed by the trees around the Place, I see the angel of Liberty, breaking its chains and spreading its light to the world: especially today, the sun strikes the metal which seems white hot. A few shards of light pierce the shadows, like so many tongues of fire descending on all the different nationalities crowding the square, one of Paris' most popular tourist destinations. Decidedly, Pentecost is not far off...

How times have changed. In Rue de la Roquette I came across a pretty little bookshop which displayed in its shop window a beautiful slogan, that I know we both appreciate: Reading is Resistance...".

Truth and Liberty

I thought over Florence's letter for several days, so that what follows could only be a reply such addressed directly to her.

You'll see, Florence, that I have written your two key words with capitals: **Truth** and **Liberty**. The idea of Liberty spreading its wings made me think, and accompanied me for several days along the Way, perhaps because of the strange sensation of freedom that comes to me from time to time, as I walk through fields and woods. And then there is the Truth, something that we seek without knowing what it is and sure only that it remains forever out of reach, a little like the goal of the pilgrimage, since on pilgrimage, if you look too hard you'll never find what you're looking for.

Liberty

I know how much you distrust the notion of "Truth" because you see in it a religious idea which justifies imposing one's "own" religious law on others (and let's not forget, of course, that there are also secular religions). But for me, it's the notion of "Liberty" that I find suspect. Did you know that George Orwell once remarked that in France, "Liberty, Equality, Fraternity" is what they put over the doors of prisons and police stations? That said, it is clear that the idea of

"Liberty" is more than just a mystification. In general, we think of it as a good, as something desirable. According to Paul Radin,[4] archaic man is fundamentally individualistic, and seeks above all to realise himself, to shine as an individual, to acquire *mana*, a Maori term meaning power, charisma, or prestige. He aims to act freely — though always according to the laws of his community — and so to win the esteem of his fellows. The notion of freedom is thus far from being unknown to him, and I deduce from this that it is an essential characteristic of man, though I cannot help wondering if it is not a singularly masculine one.

On the Camino, I am sometimes gripped by a strange sensation of liberty, of an absence of landmarks or constraints. And yet, my life on the Way is hemmed in by all kinds of constraints: the backpack to begin with, which weighs down any sudden whims; then there is the Way itself, which leads towards Compostela in stages that stretch out one after the other, measured in kilometres, stages that you have to adapt to depending on your taste and above all your strength, and the possibility or not of finding a place to stay. I am hardly "free" to do whatever might take my fancy.

(To be strictly honest, I should probably add that this sensation of freedom doubtless has something to do with the fact that I am not subject to the usual constraints of daily life: no housework, no shopping to be done, no responsibilities to anybody else, no need to answer the doorbell, and so on...)

At one point the Way ran alongside the railway line, and I saw the train from Limoges to Périgueux go past. For a moment, it seemed to me absurd to cover all this distance so slowly, and at times painfully, when I could do it in minutes, and so much more easily, just by jumping on a train. Obviously that would have negated the whole point of the journey, which was precisely to arrive on foot in Compostela.

---

4 Paul Radin, *Primitive Man as Philosopher*, 1927

Therein, doubtless, lies the answer. All these constraints did not seem to be such because I had fixed them for myself. I had chosen myself to follow the Way, and this choice imposed its constraints, which I had accepted freely because I had chosen them freely — after all, I could have stayed at home. And if you think about it, every time that you make a choice or take a decision, you choose one possible path over another, so that the freedom to take the other path no longer exists. If to be free is to make choices, then it is also to close off other ways, to accept the constraints that we impose on ourselves. So our sensation of freedom is born of the possibility of making choices which seem to us to be free ones.

But how free are they really?

The choices that I can make depend on those made by others. I could never have undertaken to walk the Way were it not for the help of all the volunteers who mark out the route or manage the hostels where I stayed. My ability freely to walk the way thus depends on the free choices made by others. Said like that, it seems obvious, incredibly banal even. But isn't it just the opposite of the usual idea that "my freedom stops where the freedom of others begins"? On the contrary, my freedom depends on that of others, and should therefore also contribute to that of others.

It is said that Socrates, when he wanted to think about a problem, would begin by asking their opinion of people he met in the street. If it worked for Socrates, I thought, why not for me? I began to ask people encountered along the Way, "What does freedom mean to you?". I have to confess that they were usually taken aback to be asked the question outright like that. Perhaps because we are constantly told that we are "free", that we live in a "free country", we end up supposing that is true and think no more about it. Anyway, the replies I got all seemed to me pretty similar, and boiled down to the idea that freedom means living as one chooses. To that was often added the idea that being free also means being able to distinguish that which is essential from that which is not. There is more than a touch of the Buddha in that idea: what pains us is not the lack of things, but the desire of things that we lack; overcome the desire, and you rid yourself of the pain.

I can't help thinking that this is both true and false.

It is certainly necessary to resist false needs, that is to say the needs imposed on us from outside by the enormous machinery of indoctrination and brain-washing that is commonly called "the media" and advertising. I remember when Patrick Lay, the director of the French commercial TV channel TF1, declared openly that his job was "to sell empty brain time to Coca-Cola". It created a scandal in the media (funnily enough!) at the time, but the real scandal was not what he said but the fact that he said it and that it was true. In fact the outcry merely served to cover the reality, which is much more insidious and difficult to perceive. At all events, and even if it's a bit superficial, I think that the people I spoke to were right to describe the needs created for us, and in a sense imposed on us, as an infringement of our freedom. And that, even if these needs are imposed by default by the destruction of all the popular cultures that once existed, with their own values that did not entirely correspond to the dominant social norms.

I was reminded of something my poet friend once told me. His parents had been refugees, who had fled the victorious Franco regime after the Spanish Civil War, and he had grown up in a poor immigrant district where the Spaniards kept alive a little cultural centre, with a library, and a place for people to meet to read, to play chess, even to put on amateur theatricals. The centre's disappearance coincided with the arrival of the television. Doubtless also with a certain improvement in material conditions which made it possible for working people to buy televisions. But the atomisation created by the television, which allows us to "amuse" ourselves without taking an active part in the amusement and without leaving home, rang the death-knell of this independent culture.

We are told that we are "free". In reality we live in a deeply totalitarian society.

The idea that we should "be content with a little" thus seems to me to express, perhaps not entirely consciously, a resistance which is perfectly valid and even necessary. Nonetheless it places us before yet another problem: just what is the "little" in question? To take an example: most of us today consider that a heated home, with a toilet, a bathroom, and hot and cold running water, is a basic necessity, but this was not always so. I grew up in a house without central heating, and when I arrived in Paris I had friends who lived in a flat regulated by the Law of 1947, without a bathroom; a generation earlier, people were content with toilets shared between several apartments, and the self-righteous bourgeois claimed that there was no point installing baths in workers' houses because they would only use them to store coal. In other words, even when our needs are physiologically based, the manner in which they are satisfied depends on the degree of culture and technical development achieved by society as a whole. Marx put it very well: the hunger of primitive man may well have been identical to ours, but there is a world of difference between a hunger assuaged by raw meat cut from the carcass of a newly killed animal on the savannah, and that satisfied by steak and chips eaten in a Parisian restaurant.

Our freedom is thus inseparable from the material level at which we live. That might seem pretty banal, after all isn't it obvious that I cannot travel without the material means to do so? I must live in a society which makes that possible and I must myself have the financial resources which allow me access to these social material means (ships, trains, places to stay, food...). A millionaire might thus seem to be freer than me. But the millionaire lives surrounded by other constraints: he can **only** travel in luxury hotels, surrounded by flunkeys at his beck and call to satisfy his every whim. The millionaire can only see the world through those who are at his service. Like me, the millionaire is enclosed in social constraints, though with a difference. What for me is a material constraint imposed by my limited means, for him is a privilege.

"To be content with little", if we don't push our reflection a little further, can thus itself become a trap, its positive transformed into a negative.

If liberty means "living as I choose", then what is it that I choose? To desire is not enough, we must know what we desire and that in turn is determined by our imagination, by our ability to imagine — that is, to picture to ourselves — what we could choose to do. And our imaginations are powerfully determined: by the material and cultural level (in the broadest sense) of the society in which we have grown up and in which we live; by our education; by the habits of social thought.

Rereading these lines, I am suddenly reminded of all those peoples, like the Plains Indians in America, who fought to be "free". This did not mean that their societies were necessarily freer than the Western society that swallowed them, but they certainly must have felt freer in them, because they could live there according to their own rules — rules which they had not perhaps chosen, but which were familiar to them, in which they were anchored historically, and which they considered their own (not to mention the fact that all these conquered peoples were subjected to racism and laws of social exclusion). Often enough, these peoples also considered Western society to be shockingly dishonest and immoral.

But to return to ourselves, and the society in which we ourselves live.

In our society, is there not a conscious effort by the ruling strata to control, imprison, chain down, and above all impoverish our imaginations? We see it concretely in the mass production of food. MacDonald's wants to sell a single product which is easy to manufacture in large quantities at minimal cost; to do so, it appeals to the elementary flavours common to all human beings and which require no gustatory education: sugar, salt, acid. In the same way, complexity, variety, originality and individuality are proscribed for the masses; or perhaps it would be closer to the mark to say that these qualities are permissible only to the extent that they can be channelled and pressed into profitable service.

Just as the MacDonald's diet deforms the human metabolism and morphology,[5] the cultural diet we are mostly fed with (have you ever noticed, by the way, how it is forbidden in TV advertising to be old, sick, or unhappy?) both expresses and reinforces the awful emotional void that has hollowed out the heart of contemporary society. And doesn't this impoverishment of our emotional resources also damage our ability to act freely?

We need to imagine a radically different society, where the development of each human being's complexity, variety, originality and individuality is a goal consciously adopted by society as a whole, and where the individual's development is a factor in social development. In the meantime, liberty will always be an act of resistance that begins with self-education. In a sense, this too is blindingly obvious: the more potential choices I can imagine, the freer I will be in my choices. To be free thus means to open oneself to others, to other individuals, to other cultures past and present, to all the richness of human history. To be free means confronting one's own prejudices, one's own mental habits; it means putting oneself in question, and this we can only really do with the help of others. Doubtless we have to accept that our degree of liberty is limited, inasmuch as our imaginations are determined. But up to a point, it is possible to increase our freedom of action by calling on our society's artistic and scientific resources, and on those of previous societies, to enlarge our imagina-

---

[5] https://www.who.int/fr/news-room/fact-sheets/detail/obesity-and-overweight

tions and call into question the chains that we forge for ourselves.

Just now I said that liberty depends on constraints, in the sense that to be free is to make choices, and each choice inevitably entails closing alternative choices. But perhaps we should push this idea a bit further? To be free does not mean doing whatever we like independently of any constraint. A person who acts without any feeling of obligation to others is a sociopath, and a sociopath is anything but free. On the contrary, he is shut up in himself, a slave to himself and to his own passions. True freedom can only exist through our relations with others and that in turn means accepting responsibility for, and even insisting on, our obligations towards others.

None of this is a matter for formal education. The educational system's goal is not to create free, independent, and critical minds, but to reproduce the existing social system which is interested in creativity only inasmuch as it can be channelled into commercial or ideological production.

…

I put what I had written to one side, but woke up the next day deeply dissatisfied with what I had written. Everything seemed confused, though there are probably some ideas hidden in it somewhere. For a moment I felt like deleting everything and starting again, but then what I am trying to do here is to seize the thinking process as it emerges, even if that means including ideas which seem opaque and inadequate, and to which, some day, I will have to return. *Alea jacta est*, then…

...

Up to now, I realise, I have only spoken of individual liberty. But this liberty is circumscribed by all the material society which surrounds it and within which it acts. The social environment — in other words, all the social relations that human beings build amongst themselves as they engage in their life processes — within which we act, is out of our control, indeed it is out of anybody's control including the powerful. We control little, if anything, of the productive system which serves to satisfy, and even to create our needs.

Humanity is divided into classes, castes, nations, and these divisions are also maintained by those who profit most from them. Think of Bastille Day, when every one of the French political parties, without exception, tells us that we are "French" and that we need a "France that is strong"; or think of Theresa May (the British Prime Minister as I write these lines) for whom "a citizen of the world is a citizen of nowhere". When I heard that, the expression immediately reminded me of another: "rootless cosmopolitan", which served as a dog-whistle for the Nazis and the Stalinists to designate Jews.

While we're on the subject of Bastille Day, I can't help thinking of Georges Brassens, who was a free spirit to the fullest extent possible in the present world, and his song "Bad reputation". In his honour, here is a flavour of the lyrics:

> *When it comes to Bastille Day*
> *In my cosy bed I stay,*
> *Music that has to march in step*
> *Never managed to get me up,*
> *Yet what harm do I do to one and all*
> *When I ignore the bugle's call?*

Because of all these divisions, and because the whole social mechanism is like an immense juggernaut gone out of control, it is impossible for us to act as free, associated individuals. It is impossible for us to fix ourselves common goals, although there is no shortage of worthwhile goals awaiting us: restoring the balance between nature and humanity, exploring the oceans and outer space, are the ones I prefer. You can surely think of others.

As long as we are not free to take part in the creation and the enactment of a collective goal determined by society as a whole, to decide together on society's rules, and to enlarge the boundaries of what it is possible to imagine, then our liberty to act is tightly constrained within a meagre and unsatisfying domain. Of course, we have to make the most of the possibilities that we have, but let us not allow ourselves to be lulled into the illusion that we are "free". How right George Orwell was, to point out that "Liberty" is inscribed, with no sense of irony, over prison gates, and yet I can't help thinking that what freedom we do have is only exercised within an enormous prison.

Truth

I can feel already that we're going to come back to this subject, since we haven't managed to agree on what Truth could be. When we spoke about it last, I understood (or misunderstood) that for you, the idea of Truth is necessarily unique and exclusive, as it is for the Catholic Church (and indeed for all kinds of sects, and not only religious ones at that), whose Pope's utterances are The Truth. If one accepts this definition clearly it is meaningless to talk of Truth. Nobody, no social structure (a church, a political party, whatever you like), can possess the whole truth. One can be more or less right of course, but that is something else entirely.

I proposed a different definition: Truth is "the best description possible of reality as a whole, at a given moment in time". You answered, I think, that for you that is reality.

I have a problem with this, and to explain why I need first to make explicit two basic premises. The first, is that there is just **one** reality, which englobes the entire universe as we know it, from the Big Bang to the present day. There are not several realities, there is no lowly Earth on the one hand, and a heavenly kingdom obeying its own rules on the other, there is no spirit realm which transcends the material world in which we live. The second (which is obvious enough, but which impressed me strongly when I first encountered the idea), is that any description of reality is itself a part of reality, but only a part. The description can thus never correspond completely to the reality, since this would be a contradiction in terms, the part encompassing the whole.

What I find beautiful and poetic in the human effort to understand the world (and which may take scientific, historical, or artistic forms) is that humans strive unceasingly towards an impossible goal: a universal description, that anyone could grasp and understand, of the entire reality of which we are a part. Is it not a beautiful thing to attempt the impossible, by perfecting our knowledge of reality, and by passing on our knowledge and the history of our attempts towards knowledge, even when they are wrong, to future generations?

Do we want to be free?

But when we talk of Liberty, another fundamental problem arises and it is this: Liberty is always presented as a desirable good, but do we really want to be free?

To be free is not merely to "do what one likes", as a child might imagine. We need to know what it is that we want, what it is possible to want, and what it is possible to achieve. Liberty imposes its own demands, and the first is, that to be free is an effort that must be renewed every day.

Engels said that to be free is to understand what is necessary, and to act on that understanding, which implies both the ability to understand what is necessary, and a will to act. It's far from easy.

In today's world, one might ask whether this much-vaunted Liberty is truly desired by many. We live in the epoch of the providential man, the extreme personalisation of public affairs, whether the person in question be a Trump, a Marine Le Pen, or indeed a Macron. Are those who want to "make America great again" ready to assume the responsibility of freedom, or do they not prefer to abandon their freedom into the hands of the President? And isn't the populism that the commentators get so worked up about just the logical consequence of the present democratic, parliamentary system? Rousseau once said that the English are only free every five years (at election time), and that the use they make of their freedom shows that they deserve to be slaves the rest of the time. In Rousseau's day, the right to vote was limited and hence also the number of voters; today, we can all vote for the members of the ruling classes who will hoodwink us until the next elections. What's saddest is that there is no shortage of people who ask nothing better than to be hoodwinked by carefully designed illusions. And so democracy turns out to be nothing more than the right to place one's own destiny into the hands of another, or rather, into the hands of a ruling elite.

Is not real freedom rather to unite the conscious and creative energy of the mass, with the individual's effort, apprenticeship, and will to act? And to achieve this, should we not envisage a truly radical reorganisation of public affairs — one, that is to say, that goes to the roots — and of our whole way of thinking?

Churches and pilgrimages

Of the wondrous doings of God most high is this, that He has created the hearts of men with an instinctive desire to seek these sublime sanctuaries, and yearning to present themselves at their illustrious sites, and has given the love of them such power over men's hearts that none alights in them but they seize his whole heart, nor quits them but with grief at separation from them (…) Intensity of yearning brings them near while yet far off, presents them to the eye while yet unseen, and makes little account to him who seeks them the fatigues which he meets and the distress which he endures.
The travels of Ibn Battuta (14th century), from the chapter on his pilgrimage to Mecca.

Nobody on the Way says "I'm going to Compostela", rather they say "I'm heading for Compostela". One must not tempt God (or the Gods, or fate, or Lady Luck, or whatever). One is never certain to arrive, indeed during the Middle Ages many were the pilgrims who died along the Way. On the journey then, Compostela can sometimes seem to exist only in the imagination, a destination ever present in mind but where one hardly dares believe one will some day arrive.

Even more than the town of Compostela, the whole pilgrimage seems somehow imaginary. The name of that far-off town, Santiago de Compostela, derives first from St James (San Iago in Spanish), and then from *Campus Stellae*, the "field of stars", since the hermit Pelagius was said to have been guided by a shower of shooting stars, in 838, to the resting place of the martyr St James. The hermit ran to find Bishop Theodomir who came straightway to examine the find, and who declared forthwith that the remains discovered in a Roman tomb were indeed those of St James, the first Christian martyr executed in the year 44. Theodomir informed King Alfonso II of the Asturias of the discovery. The king ordered the construction of a church on the spot, and himself undertook the first pilgrimage from his capital of Oviedo. His route, from Oviedo over the Asturian mountains to Compostela, by way of Lugo, gave its name to the "Camino Primitivo" (the First Way).

What were St James' remains doing in Spain? According to legend, he is supposed to have evangelised Iberia. The Holy Virgin is even said to have pushed the miraculous to its limits by sailing over to help him in a stone boat, whose remains can still be admired on the coast by Muxía. These ties with the Iberian peninsula are the reason that James' companions, after his death, brought his remains with them for burial in the lands he converted. According to some stories, the ship transporting the body nearly foundered in a storm when close to shore. Despite his decapitation, the saint kept his head and not only brought the ship safely to port but even indicated where he should be buried.

This is all, of course, highly unlikely, not to say entirely imaginary. Indeed, the first documentary evidence of the legend is the Concordia de Antealtares, which dates from 1077 and was written to assert its authenticity and therefore the privileges of the religious organisations responsible for the upkeep of the places of pilgrimage. What is beyond doubt, on the other hand, is King Alfonso's interest in the area. This was in the middle of the *Reconquista*, the long struggle to expel the Arabs from Spain, and the creation of the pilgrimage allowed the king to augment his prestige and to encourage the faithful to come and populate the region. Perhaps the gold mines, already exploited in Roman times, also had something to do with it. And if that meant inventing some relics, and the whole story that went with them, it was not for the first nor the last time. Another version of the legend even recounts that the body was discovered minus its head, and that the head was recovered later, stolen in the Holy Land by Maurice Bourdin, a Benedictine monk on his own pilgrimage to Jerusalem. More amusingly, some historians believe that the body is in reality that of the notorious heretic Priscillian.

So, St James the Imaginary… but in fact, you come across similar cases all along the Way, secondary pilgrimages so to speak.

The best known of these is Conques, on the Way from Puy-en-Velay. Frustrated that pilgrims were not stopping at the abbey, the abbot despatched one of his monks, a certain Ariviscus, to the town of Agen where the church sheltered the relics of St Foy (a person whose historicity is doubtful); after a stay of ten years, Ariviscus so gained the confidence of the population that he was able to purloin the holy relics on the evening of Epiphany, and to make off with them to Conques. Since then the abbey of Conques has profited from the pilgrimage in the most monetary terms, thanks to the gifts of all those pilgrims who stopped at the abbey on their way to Compostela, to worship the holy relics. Of course, the monks of Agen protested vehemently, but Conques replied that possession is 9/10 of the law and since then the theft has been decorously concealed under the denomination of a "pious transposition".

Another example comes from Cadouin in the Dordogne. For centuries, this magnificent abbey was the destination for pilgrims coming to adore a Holy Shroud that had once covered the body of Christ. Over the years, the pilgrimage declined, until it was revived in the 19th century. Its renewed popularity lasted until the 1930s, when a Jesuit historian came to study the Shroud and realised that the decoration embroidered around the edge consisted in reality of Arabic script. For centuries, the faithful had been worshipping a Holy Shroud inscribed in terms that are certainly holy, but hardly Christian: "Allah is great and Mohammed is his prophet". Nobody knows how the Shroud arrived in Cadouin; perhaps a knight returned from the Crusades gave it to the abbey in a sudden fit of piety. I have always wondered who swindled whom. I can well imagine a Greek or Arab merchant from Antioch swindling some naive simpleton of a crusader and selling him a Shroud, a real one, I swear on my mother's head, and for such a reasonable price… But I can equally imagine a shrewd crusader returning home and offering the supposed Shroud to the abbey to gain the absolution of his sins and the salvation of his soul at a reduced rate. And I can just as well imagine that the monks of Cadouin were not fooled, any more than some at least of the monks at Conques.

Talking of relics, on the Way from Vézelay you pass through the little town of Neuvy St Sépulchre whose church bears witness to their power of fascination. The church is strikingly odd, indeed it is unique in France, since a rotunda has been added to the altar end of the romanesque nave. The rotunda was paid for by the local lord Eudes de Déol on his return from a pilgrimage to the Holy Land; it is intended to resemble the Holy Sepulchre in Jerusalem, for it houses three precious relics, including a phial of the true blood of Christ. Did Eudes really believe in it? Impossible to say, but as a result the town of Neuvy became a secondary pilgrimage on the great Way to Compostela.

Then there is St Léonard en Noblat, an agreeable town with a pretty medieval centre and a very fine church built in granite, dedicated to the eponymous saint who is supposed to be buried there. St Léonard is a likeable saint. He is said to have been a young noble in the court of Clovis, the first King of the Franks. On his conversion to Christianity, he took an active part in the conversion of Clovis and his court. Clovis was so impressed by the young man's character that he gave him the right to set free any prisoners that he considered deserving of mercy. Rather than remain at court, the holy man preferred to retire to a modest hermitage near the village of Noblat where he was joined, over the years, by faithful followers, amongst whom were some of those he had freed from prison. His reputation only grew after his death, such that he became the patron saint of prisoners to whom prayers were offered in the hope of liberation. He was credited, notably, with the liberation of Bohémond of Antioch from a Turkish prison, after which Bohémond gave thanks by visiting Noblat and making generous gifts to the church there (Bohémond was the son of Robert Guiscard, the Norman conqueror of Apulia and Sicily).

St Léonard appears then, as a thoroughly amiable saint, who freed prisoners from their chains and (perhaps by extension?) women from the perils of pregnancy, as well as (though I have no idea why) protecting cows from disease.

There is just one problem. None of it is true. Léonard may well have existed as a local celebrity. Perhaps he was indeed a holy man, one of many hermits famous only in their own land. Or perhaps he was one of those pagan gods or spirits who underwent conversion, so to speak, and found themselves enrolled under the banners of the Christian church as saints. But there is no mention of him in the documents of Clovis' court. Indeed he is not mentioned anywhere until the 11ᵗʰ century, when Jourdain de Laron, the Bishop of Limoges, commissioned a history of Léonard's life. Jourdain had been the secular lord of Noblat and was elevated to the bishopric in 1023, and the "history" was entirely made up, in a medieval copy/paste of episodes from other holy lives. Once again, the Way saw the creation of a new pilgrimage, with its influx of the faithful and their humble offerings.

This is by no means a purely Christian phenomenon; there seems, on the contrary, to be something verging on the universal about this tendency for people whose moral qualities were admired in their lifetime to become objects of veneration after their death, until little by little the story of their real lives merges with other qualities and other, even supernatural, beings and stories. Their true origins are forgotten and they acquire the status of immortal sainthood. In his *Travels*, the 14th century jurist Ibn Battuta gives many such examples from the world of Islam. In China, one of the most popular saints is Guan Yu (or Guandi), who was a historical figure of the Three Kingdoms period. He served as a general under Liu Bei and Cao Cao and was much admired for his courage, loyalty, honesty and general moral probity. So much so that after his death he became a popular figure of veneration, and finally both the Taoist God of War, and a *boddhisatva* in the Buddhist tradition. On the distaff side, the most popular goddess in China is Guanyin, who started out in real life as a benevolent woman of means from a coastal village. She looked after sailors and fisherman who had suffered shipwreck or other difficulties in life, and ended up as a *boddhisatva* and the Goddess of Mercy and Compassion, as well as being the patron saint of sailors and fishermen. It is worth noting the role played in all these cases, by the royal adoption and promotion of saintly figures admired by the population as a whole; should we not see this as a means of coopting the moral attributes of the saint to the benefit of the king or emperor and his aristocracy?

I've only scratched the surface here, and I confess that all these saintly stories encountered along the Way leave me perplexed. How far did those men and women of the Middle Ages believe in them? The use of fake histories and documents was commonplace. One of the best known was the so-called "Donation of Constantine" which was supposedly a document from the reign of Constantine giving temporal power over the Roman Empire in the West to Pope Silvester. The document's provenance is unknown, but for several centuries it served the Papacy to justify the Church's tremendous wealth, as well as its attempts to exert political rule over Europe's kings and princes. And it is far from being the only example.

It would be easy enough to attribute all this to the cynicism of the ruling classes, but this seems to me much too simplistic. The epoch, after all, was steeped in religious belief. Despite — or rather because of — their misdeeds, the great really did fear for their salvation, their belief was not just a smokescreen for the benefit of the exploited. Otherwise, how are we to explain the sometimes extravagant gifts to the Church, of land especially, to the point where, when Henry VIII of England broke with Rome and seized the Church's goods, almost a third of the country's land belonged to it. Often, especially at the end of the Middle Ages after the Black Death had killed between a third and a half of the European population, gifts of land were associated with the construction of extravagant chapels in the cathedrals, and intended to finance monks to sing prayers for the soul of the deceased, for all eternity, in the hope of reducing its time in Purgatory.

Have things changed so much since then? I can't help thinking of all those immensely wealthy 19th century industrialists, men like Dale Carnegie or Henry Clay Frick. They amassed enormous fortunes in the steel industry thanks to the ferocious exploitation of their workforce, only to devote a large part of them to educational or artistic foundations. Was that enough to buy them a clean conscience?

I have seen the Pyrenees!

St Jean Pied de Port, where all the French Ways come together before heading over the Pyrenees, had been a goal in my mind for so long that the idea of actually arriving there had begun to seem unreal. And yet, on one fine and sunny day, on the heights of the Béarn just before I walked down into Orthez, I saw them at last in the distance: the Pyrenees!

I hadn't intended to detail each stage of my journey — so many have done so already, what could I add to their accounts? And yet having walked through so many changes of place and countryside, each one with its share of impressions and encounters, it seems wrong just to sweep them aside as if they had left no mark on my mind. The Way ends up imposing its own rhythm, even on the written word. After leaving Nevers I walked more than 800km and passed through Berry, the Nivernais, the Limousin, the Bergerac, the Bordelais, the Landes and the Béarn, to arrive at last in St Jean Pied de Port in the heart of the Basque Country. France offered me one of its most remarkable characteristics: so much diversity in so little space.

Strange to say, I hadn't noticed that proliferation of church-reliquaries that had so intrigued me on the road to Périgueux, and that I described in the previous chapter.

Not that there aren't any churches, on the contrary, they are many and beautiful. There are castles too in abundance, since much of the Way lies along the front line between English and French during the Hundred Years War and even before. It was a long struggle that began in the 12th century with the marriage of Henry II Plantagenet, King of England, to Eleanor of Aquitaine; the English arrived and understandably didn't want to leave. The history of their presence remains vivid in these regions, in the buildings but also more intangibly in local tradition. One day, when I stopped in the village of Argelos to buy raspberries (after a stiff climb which proved a fore-taste of the Pyrenees to come), the farmer informed me that the village was one of several, even including the town of Hagetmau which I had just left, first established by Henry II as strongholds. You can see it in the churches, which are so often built to serve for both prayer and defence. And nowhere will you see it more clearly than in Sauveterre-de-Béarn, where the legendary Gaston Fébus, Count of Béarn and of Foix, remains almost tangibly present.

It's a strange sensation, this constant to and fro between the past and the present, between a medieval world seen at a walker's pace, and the modern world imprinted in the shapes of the fields and the techniques of agriculture with their gigantic farm machines that occasionally rumble past you, as well as the social emptiness encountered so often in the little country towns.

What a remarkable woman Eleanor of Aquitaine must have been. I am certain that it was she who inspired the bawdy words of the *Carmina Burana*:

> *Were diu werlt alle min von deme mere unze an den Rin des wolt ih*
> *mih darben, daz diu chunegin von Engellant lege an minen armen.*
> *(If all the world were mine, from the sea down to the Rhine, I would*
> *give it all up just to hold the Queen of England in my arms)*

Beautiful, shrewd, well-educated, a patron of the arts who grouped around her person a rich court of artists and troubadours, certainly an inspiration for the ideas of courtly love… You think I'm exaggerating? Not so much, surely: her legend would not have come down to us had there not been some truth to it. At all events, she has left us a more attractive memory than that of her husband who is best known in history for the murder of his erstwhile friend Thomas à Becket, the Archbishop of Canterbury assassinated before the altar in his own cathedral. Oh and by the way, since we were talking of relics and pilgrimages, the one to Canterbury to pray on the relics of the martyred saint and archbishop was England's most important and gave birth to the first real masterpiece of English literature: Chaucer's *Canterbury Tales*.

I think back too, to Gaston Fébus. Johan Froissart, the chronicler of the Hundred Years War, said of him:

> *I have seen many knights, kings and princes. But I never saw one of*
> *such magnificent stature and such imposing presence. His face was very*
> *beautiful, bright and full of laughter. His eyes were green and loving.*
> *He was perfect in every way. He loved what it was right that he should*

In an age when disease struck down both lord and labourer, and left the body marked and scarred, it is hardly surprising that people noticed and valued the strength and beauty of youth, so conscious were they of its fleeting and fragile nature. And like Eleanor, Gaston was not only handsome but intelligent: a great military leader and an astute strategist who played on the rivalry between the kings of France and England in order to maintain his own independence and to avoid being caught up in their royal wars. You can already see here the disintegration of the feudal principle according to which everyone held their lands in fief from a single lord, since Gaston was in principle, at one and the same time a vassal of the Kings of England, France, and Aragon, all of whom had every interest in treating with him cautiously to keep him from passing overtly into the opposing camp.

You might think that my somewhat romantic (not to say sentimental) predilection for this epoch and its colourful characters tends to obscure the oppression of the peasants who produced the wealth that the rich lords spent, and the journeymen artisans who built the castles and cathedrals. Not so! But we cannot judge an epoch by the criteria of our own. All is movement, every social form — because it is a living form, like the men and women who compose it and who make the choices through which it develops — is born, lives, and must die. The important thing is whether it allowed a new and higher social form to germinate within it.

...

Walking again: what a difference separates today from the pilgrim of the Middle Ages!

First of all, there is the relationship between those who walk the

Way and those who see them pass by. Once, it was the pilgrim on the Way who brought news from afar, from the countries he had passed through. Today, it's the opposite; unless the pilgrim makes the effort to read the newspaper he keeps with him to stuff in his boots and dry them out of an evening, he is cut off from the world of TV news and indeed news of any kind. I only learnt of the terrible bomb attack in Manchester by accident, because it was on the TV news in the bar where I stopped for coffee before leaving La Châtre.

And then, there's the matter of speed. In the Middle Ages, the world turned at a pedestrian speed. Everyone went on foot, and even the best mounted horseman could hardly ride at a constant gallop. Today, to see the world pass you by at a walker's pace makes you realise just how much your world is slowed down compared to everybody else's. In the countryside, everyone gets around by car. The farmer checks up on his fields by quad or SUV, the harvest is taken in by tractor, adolescents zoom around on scooters, and even the slowest ride a bicycle. The pilgrim meanwhile can only advance at the rhythm of one foot after another, kilometre after kilometre.

The most extreme of contrasts. Walking through the Forest of the Landes, I heard from time to time the furious roar of a fighter jet; the Air Force uses the Landes for low-altitude training from the aerodrome at Mont-de-Marsan. I didn't actually see the plane until I reached a stretch of the path unencumbered by trees. It flew low, flashing by me at an unimaginable speed before arrowing up into the sky where seconds later it was no more than a barely visible dot, leaving only the thunder of its engines behind it. I thought of everything that separated me from the unknown pilot: him, the master of the ultimate expression of modern technology, covering in moments a distance that would demand several days of walking; me, an heir to a long-gone epoch, with the desire at least to express thereby a refusal of everything that the pilot and his fighter plane stand for. Yet, when it comes down to it, I am no less dependent on modern technology than he is, from the waterproofing in my boots to my ultra-light rain gear and my Osprey Anti-gravity backpack (I really love that back-pack, I can't resist going on about it…). Even more extraordinary, there's my mobile phone where I store all my maps and which shows me, at a mere tap of the finger, exactly where I am to the nearest metre. Behind this gesture, which seems so simple and has become so automatic, there are satellites encircling the Earth with an invisible belt, a whole vast industry of satellite-launchers, and Einstein's General Relativity, so disconcerting and contrary to our intuitive awareness of the world.

So in the end, the pilot and I are part of the same world full of contradictions, though doubtless we would have difficulty in finding common ground in our view of how it turns…

From the Bordelais to Bilbao

Here I am in Bilbao, and here, for the moment, my journey ends. Family obligations have called me unexpectedly to England. Time to go back over the Way I have walked, and to try to set my ideas in some kind of order. Time, above all, to pass from one world to another.

Now that the reality confronts me, I realise that it will not be so easy to get used to no longer walking the Way. No more getting up at 05:30 in the morning to load the backpack, no more days spent outdoors and in the countryside, no more changing acquaintances and surroundings every day, no longer being obliged every day to open myself to new encounters, no more sleeping in a different place each night, no more sharing the sleeping space with strangers...

It's only on arriving here that I understood why those who have already walked the Camino speak of it like a virus. Personally, I would say more like a drug... this strange sensation of liberty along with an exhilarating physical well-being.

Whatever, I am certain that I will return to Bilbao to finish the Way, and as soon as possible.

I've crossed France from Vézelay to St Jean Pied de Port, then the French and Spanish Basque Countries, I've walked through heatwaves and torrential downpours. You get philosophical about it after a while: on the Way, there's nothing to be done about the weather, you just have to go forward and accept what life offers.

The same holds true for the encounters along the Way. Who will you have to cope with every evening in the next hostel? In a situation where you sleep every night in a dormitory and where you can find yourself with a perfect stranger no more than an arm's length away, a certain lack of intimacy cannot be avoided. You sometimes meet those who try to do so, you recognise them straight away by the way they sit off to one side, surrounding themselves with a wall of silence. Not unpleasant, nor arrogant, but ill at ease, too used to keeping their own company perhaps.

Personally, I'm ill at ease with my own prejudices. More than once have I found someone getting on my nerves merely because they ruffled my susceptibility, or, still more banal, my habits, my ways of doing things. In such situations, if you gave in to your prejudices life with others would quickly become intolerable. The only solution is to open up, to talk, to listen, and to try to better understand the other. Like the Dutchwoman I met in Roquefort (not the Roquefort where they make the cheese, much to my disappointment), ten years my junior, and with the solid physique typical of Dutch peasants, whose manners I found all the more bizarre because she wanted to take part in a French conversation though speaking no French. How do you join a group (especially a small one) and take part in its conversation when you don't speak the language? She had her own way of doing things which I confess to have found disconcerting, even improper. My prejudices were already on the alert, and they unhesitatingly manned the battlements as soon as I discovered that she was a prison warden. Let's just say that it is a job for which I don't feel an instinctive sympathy. But the Way has the habit of forcing encounters on you: to my surprise (she normally walked much faster than me), we found ourselves alone together in the same hostel and the discussion opened up, especially the evening when we enjoyed a shared enthusiasm for the hostel at Orthez. According to legend, the chronicler Johan Froissart (I mentioned him a few pages back) stayed there in

1388; back then, it was already called the "Hôtel de la Lune", just as it is today. It was built with defence in mind, with a fine spiral staircase to make attack more difficult.

To hell then with my prejudices. We are all human beings after all, are we not? How does one become a prison warden, I wondered? I learnt that my fellow pilgrim was born into a family of ten children (in the 1960s, that must surely be a peasant family), and that she had worked above all with plants, first in nurseries and then in a flower shop. After a while she had had enough of plants, she wanted to work with people. But why in prisons? Pure chance: she had seen a job advertised, it was in the civil service — offering a job security and a pension not to be sniffed at — so why not? And on the whole, she was not unhappy with her choice. She had begun in a women's prison, then applied for a transfer to a men's prison (apparently this is possible in Holland). It struck me that she preferred working in the men's prison. Women, she said, are too complicated: "With the women, when there's a fight and you finally get to the bottom of what started it, it turns out to be about a dispute over cigarettes several months before. With men it's much more straightforward, they yell at each other, then they hit each other, and then it's finished". To be honest I really didn't know what to make of this. Impossible to generalise from it of course, but it intrigued me nonetheless.

And so the Way works its chemistry and two people separated by their upbringing, their ideas, just about everything in fact, learn if not to know the other, at least to appreciate the other's human qualities. And when we parted for the last time, at St Jean Pied de Port where she was heading straight over the Alps on the Camino Francés, it was with real emotion that we wished each other well on the Way.

Both of us had been struck, also, by the sad condition of the villages and little country towns that we passed through. The situation wasn't the same everywhere. When you walk, you cross the countryside slowly and you have time to notice the differences between regions. The Périgord, for example, seemed to be richer, the villages better kept and surrounded by quite wealthy country houses. I put this down to the region's specialities: *foie gras*, preserved duck or goose, truffles. These are all products with a high added value for low volumes, demanding considerable manpower. But you can't live just on *foie gras* with truffles, you need wheat and meat for the hamburger industry…

Then there was the Bergerac, and a little corner of the Bordelais — a region that produces the less prestigious *crus* and is thus highly mechanised. I crossed them under a leaden sun, and got into the habit of rising at 05:00 in the morning to be on the Way by dawn, the only way to avoid walking for hours with the thermometer at 38°.

As a younger married man, I used to go regularly to the Côtes du Rhône where my wife's family lived. I found the vineyards there charming. But they seem much less so today. To be sure, you still see, here and there, the fine chateaux of the wineries. One night, the hostel even turned out to be in a winery and the three of us that stayed there were royally served of both the flesh and the vine. There is wealth there, and you certainly need a good deal of capital and a certain amount of labour to make it all work. But at what price? Vines from horizon to horizon, nothing but vines, and not so much as a patch of shade, for it is out of the question that the slightest shadow should fall on the precious grapes: no hedges, no spinneys or copses. And when it's not vines, then it's sunflower or maize as far as the eye can see. Then there are the towns, which should be pretty, which are often finely built in stone with handsome buildings and agreeable streets, where the Town Hall has done its utmost to embellish the centre and make it more lively. But there's nothing for it, there are always the empty shopfronts and the signs announcing "For Sale", which are only rarely transformed into "Sold". The young people seem to be just hanging about, and you guess that they have no work, or at least no stable work nor any perspective of having any, and you wonder what they do with themselves in these towns practically emptied of their old commercial and cultural activity.

Wealth and poverty are not just in striking contradiction, it is the wealth of the hyper-mechanised farms which is directly responsible for the misery of the country towns and their populations' flight to the major industrial and commercial cities. How could it be otherwise? The whole of agriculture, like industry, is gripped in the vice of ferocious competition, and the only response is always the same: cost reduction, reduced labour costs and manpower, mechanisation. How else could French wine compete with the wines from South Africa, Australia, or Chile, on the British market, the biggest wine importer in Europe?

. . .

We city-dwellers often have a romantic, not to say romanticised vision of country life. There, we think, people are closer to nature and to their neighbours, there is more solidarity, human relationships are more closely woven, and more human. But nothing in human existence is without ambivalence and contradictions; these relationships are subjected to what Marx called "the idiocy of rural life", where everybody knows everything about their neighbours, where a truly intimate private life barely exists, and where people are trapped in the narrowness of their limited social horizons. One day, I saw up close this social poverty which has nothing to do with the capitalisation of agriculture. Three of us pilgrims arrived together, not, exceptionally, in a hostel managed by the municipality or an association, but in a private home where a devout couple welcomed passing pilgrims, offering bed and breakfast, and an evening meal, at a modest price. Everything was charming: the house was all in the old style, the meals copious, and the elderly peasant couple strong Catholics and benevolent towards pilgrims; we were to learn later that the other members of the congregation considered them a "charming" couple, and with us they certainly were.

But between themselves! At table, they were constantly at each others' throats; even the presence of three strangers did nothing to hold them back. Biting remarks and gratuitous aggression filled the time — how much must there have been of accumulated frustration, petty little hatreds piled one on the other? Clearly, in such a traditionally religious couple divorce was out of the question, in a peasant family you can't split the property, and in a village everyone is watching your every move. Such a marriage could only be a prison whose walls they built themselves, cemented by gossip: Christian observance devoid of charity towards others, and above all towards those closest to one.

I left the next morning with a profound feeling of both relief and sadness. I hope I didn't show it, I would not want to add to the bitterness and disappointment haunting the house. I wished them well, but what hope could there be for people who built their own hell on Earth, in the expectation of an illusory Paradise in the hereafter?

The evening also afforded us a glimpse of how the rural economy works. The elderly peasant still farmed a hectare or so of vines and delivered his harvest to the local cooperative. He served us as much wine as we could drink; we were still in the Bordelais and though the wine was hardly a *grand cru* it was honest and thoroughly drinkable. He explained that the cooperative sold the wine at less than €2 the litre. Forty years ago, I used to buy Côtes du Rhône at the cooperative wineries for 7FF the litre, and if we consider that a franc then was worth roughly a euro today, then I could see how far the price to the small producer must have fallen. When you think of the manpower involved in wine production, how can one live with prices so low? There is only one way: out and out mechanisation and economies of scale, methods which of course are impossible for small producers. And if one were to increase prices to the point where small producers could survive (and, one might add in passing, to a point where city-dwellers could enjoy fruit and vegetables tasting of something more than water), then it would increase food prices and wages would have to rise correspondingly. And at least since the abolition of Britain's tariffs on imported wheat back in 1832, the "low price" of food (which the Sainsbury's, Tescos, and Walmarts of this world boast about in endless advertising) has never been anything but a means for the industrialists to keep down the cost of labour. I had the dubious pleasure of tasting the inevitable result in La Souterraine where I bought cheese and dried sausage at the Aldi discount, the only shop close to the campsite where I had settled for two days; they were so bad that I overcame my almost congenital and puritanical distaste for throwing food away, and tossed them both in the bin.

•••

Nature is less gloomy when the landscape itself sets limits on agriculture. In the Landes, to start with. The poor quality of the sandy soil means that the Landes, and the Forest of the Landes especially, has always been one of the most sparsely populated regions of France. I undertook the Way through the Forest with some trepidation. It is inexorably flat, and what's more the Way follows an old railway line so that it runs not just flat but dead straight for three full days, at least. My pains along the Canal de Berry came forcefully back to mind.

But in the end, crossing the Landes enchanted me. It started just after Bazas. I walked alone with my thoughts for company, meeting barely a living soul. I rediscovered the hypnotic quality of the Canal de Berry, as it ran straight ahead beneath my feet, but stronger still. There were no canal locks, nor anything else to mark the distance.

75

Most of the time, there was only the forest in front, behind, and around me.

And then, the silence.

It was neither hot nor cold. The trees protected me from the sun, but the weather was uncertain, it threatened to rain but it never did. For kilometres, for hours, I advanced through a forest that seemed constantly changing yet always the same.

On the second day, I came to the hamlet of Bourriot. The forest opened up into a broad clearing, then fields, and at last the menacing storm broke giving way to vast skies where the clouds piled themselves up, joined together then broke up again to create new forms: mountains, castles, dreamlike landscapes. Colour was reduced to its simplest elements: the rich brown of ploughed earth, the almost fluorescent green of an unending expanse of potato plants, the darker green of the trees, and then greys and whites of every imaginable tone, piling up in the sky.

Bourriot itself reminded me of Australia. None of the narrow lanes typical of a medieval village, nor the more ordered and rectangular streets of a modern town, here the houses were scattered about as if by chance, or according to the whims of their inhabitants. Most only boasted a ground floor, and always with a veranda over the front door, which made me think of the verandas that surround Australian houses. Same cause, same effects: in Australia there's plenty of space, you can spread yourself about, and here it's the same. I found the colours agreeable, too: often the shutters are painted a delicate shade of blue, almost violet. In fact I found everything here agreeable. Even the hamlet's deserted atmosphere didn't bother me; hardly surprising, after all, in such a sparsely populated region.

And then, I was lucky with my hosts for the evening in Bourriot, a couple from Alsace who had moved there some fifteen years previously. They were intelligent and cultured people, who had been youth workers in Alsace but had given up in disgust at the role they were obliged to play, of merely applying sticking plaster to wounds that everyone knew — without daring to say it out loud — were incurable, merely to make sure that the streets did not explode in the faces of the privileged. In Bourriot, they farmed a small market garden, based on the techniques of permaculture using plants adapted to the terrain and local to the area. They didn't expect to change the world — they had no illusions about that — but simply to find a way of life that suited them better. They told me they organised discussions inspired by the Alsatian practice of the *Stamm tisch*, a sort of open meeting held in cafés, which reminded me of the early days of the workers' movement in Britain, where the early unions and political groups would meet in pubs, the only public space that workers had open to them. The children too, their son amongst them, had organised a discussion around the theme "What is happiness?".

We talked until late. Their experience in the tough housing estates

had rendered them impervious to all the ambient hysteria over ji-
hadism, which they saw as a consequence of the social rejection felt
by children as they are growing up, the fact that nobody believes
them capable of anything, that they are given no responsibility in life.
A paradox of society today this one: everyone is alone, severed from
the social ties that once surrounded us, and gave duties and responsibilities to each individual, everyone is supposed to be "Master of my
destiny / And captain of my soul"; yet at the same time, those who
prove unable to make their way in an ever more demanding world of
work are treated like children and "aided" by a huge apparatus of social workers and miserly handouts. When society tells people that
they are basically worthless, and that there is no place for them in the
orgy of consumption that advertising invites us daily to enjoy, then is
it really surprising that they react violently? Is it really surprising that
there are those who, rather than elbowing their way to the table,
prefer to upset it?

We spoke of Liberty, and the relationship between individual and
social liberty, of freedom of action.

What did freedom mean for archaic humans, the hunter-gatherers
who are our common ancestors? Perhaps simply to live according to
their customs and wander at the ease over a territory that they felt
tied to, that indeed they felt themselves a part of because their ancestors were buried there from time immemorial.

What about us, descended for millennia from settled populations,
and for centuries from people whose civilisation has been essentially
urban, and for decades from people reliant on industrial technology?
I was impressed by their efforts to use permaculture techniques,
which both adapt themselves to the soil and try to improve it. All that
demands a sophisticated knowledge of the local ecosystem. They
were certainly intelligent enough to realise that whatever Liberty one
might achieve at the individual and local level is all too limited. You
realise quickly enough that this effort to live closer to the natural

world (which I understand and respect, even if my own garden is nothing more than a balcony in the Parisian suburbs to which I confess I pay little attention) depends on things which have become so indispensable to us that we barely notice them except when they stop working. Simple things: running water, sewage, electricity; and, I would be tempted to add, access to the Internet which has become so vital for our contact with the rest of the world, for our culture and our instruction.

These three (or four, as you wish) elements of modern life, and Liberty, all demand a considerable infrastructure: for water, a whole distribution system of water pipes, water purification facilities, and sewage works; for electricity, power stations and energy sources, a network of cables and pylons; the Internet, itself dependent on electricity, demands an enormous world wide infrastructure of computers and telecommunications. Behind these technologies lies everything necessary to build them: construction machines, mines (iron ore, rare earths, copper, etc, etc), and factories to produce the necessary tools, from the tiniest electronic component to the monstrous drilling platforms in the oil fields. And of course these are not dead technologies, since no technology can be set in motion without the presence of human beings, tens if not hundreds of thousands of workers who dig the ditches, who mine, who drill, who manufacture, or who develop software, and who keep the whole thing organised. Thus, each little bit of individual liberty is the fruit of the masses' creative action. In general, this creative action is hidden from us, even from those of us who are part of it, since each one sees only the little part that he or she deals with from day to day (having passed a good part of my life developing and installing software, I'm only too well aware of the fact). Yet at the same time, when you think about it, you realise that our "territory" is no longer the limited domain of our hunter-gatherer ancestors, but the whole planet and that, when it comes down to it, Liberty can only be conceived as a conscious participation in the collective life and organisation of all humanity. Which shows how far we are from being truly free.

We spoke of society's perspectives — or lack thereof — a subject that constantly comes up in conversation as soon as it concerns the social situation. A question that remains without an answer, leaving us prey to perplexity.

• • •

After the Landes, came the Béarn. The country became hillier, undulating under a brilliant sun. It was here, topping a rise, that I first caught sight of the Pyrenees in the distance. I was gripped by such a sense of exhilaration that I lifted my arms to the heavens and shouted for joy. On leaving Vézelay, the Pyrenees had seemed so far away that I hardly dared so much as imagine that I would see them one day. Now that I could see them for real, I knew that St Jean Pied de Port was only a few more days walking away. After that would come the mountains, and Spain — but I had said to myself long before that if ever I reached the Pyrenees, then I would be capable of anything. And now, I was there, or nearly there.

I don't know if the farming in the Béarn is less industrialised, but at all events the terrain itself imposes more variety. The rolling hills lend themselves less readily to immense expanses of mechanised monoculture. There are more cattle, and so more pasture, scattered among the woods and fields of wheat. At Sauveterre, I put up my tent in a pretty little campsite next to a swift-running, chattering river; I even took the opportunity for a dip in the cold clear water.

I walked up to the medieval town where I tried out a new way to visit churches, reserved for those where your steps resonate as soon as you walk in, and where the slightest movement seems to echo up and fill the whole nave. I've downloaded to my phone (it really does do everything), music by Hildegard von Bingen, the 12th century mystic and doctor. I place the phone on the steps before the altar and let the bewitching music, these incredibly pure female voices, rise into the church and fill it entirely. Then I retire to the back of the church, filled with wonder at the genius of the composer, and of those artisans who could build such a church, itself a veritable musical instrument made of stone capable of making the sound from my phone's tiny speakers reverberate throughout its vast expanse.

After Sauveterre, little by little the rolling hills of the Béarn gave way to the steeper slopes of the Basque Country. The countryside is more spectacular, the vistas broader.

The weather was fine, and warm. At St Palais, I stopped for coffee at a café, sitting at a table outside in the street. Around me people chatted, stopped to greet each other, the little supermarket next door smelt of melon, the streets were narrow and shady, the shutters almost all painted red and half closed. It felt like Spain already.

I made my way towards the Basque village of Ostabat, the last stop before St Jean Pied de Port. On the road I came across a stone tablet announcing the merger of the Ways from Vézelay and Puy-en-Velay, then I attacked a long rise towards a distant hilltop, on a path of bare stone and gravel that slipped away under my feet. The more I climbed the hotter it seemed to become, but I had learned long before that there is only one way to cope with the heat: slow down to avoid tiring yourself out, and go on putting one foot in front of the other.

I had been told that the Way from Vézelay is called the Way of Solitude because it is so little frequented (1700 pilgrims a year compared to the 20,000 who come from Puy-en-Velay), but I had not given any thought to what that might imply. At the top of the hill, where the grateful pilgrim discovers a little chapel and its spring of fresh water, I was astonished to encounter half a dozen people, clearly pilgrims like myself, relaxing in the shade of a few scattered trees.

Where on Earth could they have come from? The answer was obvious when I thought about it: from the Way of Puy-en-Velay. Henceforth, no more of the Way's solitude nor of the little hostels that nightly welcomed groups of three or four pilgrims at the most.

But neither this gathering at La Chapelle, nor the group of pilgrims encountered at the agreeable little bar at the entrance to Ostabat, nor the hostel there, at least twice the size of anything I had seen before, nor the dozen people sitting down for supper in the same hostel, regaled by mine host with traditional Basque songs delivered in a splendid baritone, none of all this had prepared me for my arrival at St Jean Pied de Port.

The four of us stepped boldly through the St James' Gate, for centuries the pilgrims' entrance to the town, almost like old friends; and yet, we had only met that very day on the Way. This ease with which you meet people is one of the Way's most disconcerting (or should I say seductive?) qualities. It sometimes reminds me of the atmosphere in the youth hostels where I stayed in my (much) younger days, when I went hiking in England or Wales. How can that be?

I have the impression (I don't know whether it's true for everyone or just for me) that you make friends, or at least you meet people, more easily when you're younger. Everything in life is more fluid, and that starts with both your own personality and that of others of your own age: the character is still being moulded by life, its contours are less pronounced, one is not without prejudices of course, but one's way of being in the world is less fixed. Ageing means accumulating choices and their consequences: one hopes to acquire wisdom (though that is far from guaranteed: as Georges Brassens used to sing, "Quand on est con, on est con"), but perhaps at the price of doors closed by the choices one has made. Getting older means accumulating distance, and the scars of old injuries. When you're young, you're like a curious puppy that sticks its nose into everything; with the years, you become more wary. Tragic I know, but life's like that. That's why I told myself, many years ago, that I didn't want to lose completely the naive side of youth, which sees every day anew, and fresh. Have I succeeded? I couldn't say. At all events, I don't want to look at the world with jaded, disillusioned eyes.

On the Way, it's disconcertingly easy to meet people, to start a discussion, even to reveal yourself. Doubtless because the encounter is without ties and without commitments. You can recount your life to a stranger without fear of gossip precisely because you are strangers. Generally, I walked alone: "everyone has their own rhythm" is an expression you'll hear often on the Way. But then you meet up again in the hostels, in the "*albergues*" in Spain, which makes it possible to return to the discussions of the previous evening, to explore the other. And so relationships develop little by little, fleeting perhaps but each one contributing a little knowledge of the world and the other, each one forcing the demolition of prejudice.

And so I entered at last within the walls of St Jean Pied de Port, following in the footsteps of all those pilgrims who for centuries rested here before adventuring across the Pyrenees. I recall an elderly couple, met one day during a heatwave. When I knocked on their door to ask for water, they invited me in, gave me coffee and biscuits, and told me how they had walked the Way themselves, back in the 1980s when it was a rare achievement. They had walked through such a terrible storm in the Pyrenees that, on their arrival at Puente de la Reina, the priest had said a special Mass of thanksgiving for their safe arrival. The risk is smaller nowadays, with 200-400 pilgrims leaving the town every day in the high season, though the crossing is still not to be taken lightly.

The first thing to strike me was the different populations strolling through the main street of this pretty little town which still has a medieval feel to it. First, there are the pilgrims like myself, with several hundred kilometres under their boots. They are tanned by life in the open, by the sun and the wind, not entirely clean, loaded with packs that little by little have taken on something of their owner's personality, in high spirits as if they can hardly believe they are there. Then there are the tourists, who you can spot straight away: they're too clean for one thing, after all this time on the Way I wasn't used to seeing people dressed in that dressed-up "casual" style; most of them looked to me overweight as well. They stare at the pilgrims, you can feel it, it was almost like being the dust-caked cowboy entering Hicksville in a Western, striking fear into honest townsfolk.

There were the pilgrims newly arrived by train from Bayonne. I should have realised, a lot of people start the pilgrimage at St Jean, before heading off along the Camino Francés towards Santiago. For many, it's their first time, and they gaze about them with a bewildered air.

Then of course there were the townspeople, busy like their ancestors for centuries before them with the holy work of separating the pilgrim from his money. I was reminded abruptly of a discussion in the hostel run by the St James Association in Périgueux, where several seasoned pilgrims who had all walked the Way more than once, bewailed the "touristification" of the Way, both on the side of all the businesses that profited from it, and on the side of the pilgrims themselves. But in the Middle Ages too, the pilgrimage was a business, as you can see from the quantity of relics along the Way, all of them perfectly fraudulent and sometimes even stolen, as at Conques. And after all, all those pilgrims had to be fed, lodged, and sometimes looked after. So has the town of St Jean lived for centuries, and to this day, thanks to the pilgrimage. As for the pilgrims, clearly it has become something of a fashion, you need only consult the statistics showing the impressive increase in the numbers registering each year in Compostela. If those I spoke to are a representative sample, then very few undertake the Way for religious reasons, which doesn't mean that they are not engaged in their own, intimate quest. Even if it's just for a holiday, as it was for quite a few of the young people I met in Spain, it's surely no accident that they choose to walk the Way rather than do something else. They too are seeking on the Way, the camaraderie, the encounters with the other, that are so often and so cruelly lacking in our modern lives.

Even in the Middle Ages, an epoch so much more religious than our own, there were — so it seems — professional pilgrims. The lord unable to leave his lands, the merchant unable to abandon his business, but still obliged to do penance for some misdeed by traveling to Compostela, could hire a professional who would walk the pilgrimage on their behalf. Everything could be bought after all, you could even buy Indulgences to reduce the time spent in Purgatory — so why not the penitence of pilgrimage as well?

•••

On leaving St Jean, I had intended to follow the crests of the Pyrenees as far as the coast and to pick up the Camino del Norte at Irun, which is the first town on the Spanish side of the border. The Pilgrims' Office at St Jean advised against it: the paths were slippery, the summits hidden in the clouds, in these conditions the GR10 can be perilous for a heavily loaded walker; worse still, a storm was blowing up and the mountain tops are dangerous in a thunderstorm. The *hospitalero* proposed an alternative route through the foothills. I didn't regret it.

The Basque Country seduced me completely. The countryside reminded me of Wales (especially when it was cloudy — perfect for the walker). The hills lapped against the mountains that rose, wild and romantic, inaccessible above the fields and pastures; on the summits, rocks were jumbled together in what the Welsh and the Cornish call a tor; the sheep were little white dots grazing on the rich green grass; the Basque houses were all painted white, scattered here and there in the folds of the hills. Even the clouds delighted me, protecting me from the sun and lending the countryside a dramatic and constantly moving aspect. I liked the houses from close up too, similar to those I had seen in the Landes, with pleasant balconies sheltered under overhanging roofs. They were invariably spick and span, painted in white, with shutters painted red or green (the colours of the Basque flag, of course). The Basques like stone and wood, the doors and windows were all surrounded by good stone and imposing beams, even the modern ones which are mostly built with breeze blocks. Sometimes, this brings to mind the whimsical image of a sort of popular conspiracy, as if everybody had agreed to transform the landscape into an immense collective sculpture.

And I liked the Basque churches. I had been told that the Basques love to sing — again like the Welsh, who have a great choral tradition — and it shows in the churches, all equipped with splendid wooden galleries for the choir, made in dark wood and sometimes rising three levels above the congregation, a heavenly chorus it must have been indeed. Sometimes a model of a three-masted schooner hung from the rafters — but I never discovered why.

...

The first day out from St Jean found me at Bidarray, where I experienced a sort of physical epiphany. The day had not been a long one, only 22km, but I had crossed over two passes and the countryside was the hilliest I had encountered so far. Arriving in the village, I sat down to a beer at the café, and was suddenly possessed by a feeling of intense physical wellbeing. It wasn't an absence of fatigue, rather a powerful sensation of the entire body functioning as it should, a sense of the unity of all the body's limbs and organs, of their perfect integration with the mind. When first I set out, I dreaded arriving in a town at the end of a day's walk, and finding myself with kilometres more to go before I reached my night's lodging; but on that day, my body told me I could quite happily do five or six kilometres more without batting an eyelid.

At the time, I put the feeling down to chance: the body changes all the time, the sensation of one's "vital spirit" ready to confront physical effort is more or less present. But I was mistaken: the same sensation stayed with me and even increased in power, day after day.

It reminded me of the intoxication of long-distance runners by the accumulation of endorphins in the brain. Doubtless, it owed something to the previous 800km: it would be surprising if my body had not adapted to the rhythm I had imposed on it. Training probably bears fruit less quickly as we get older, nonetheless I can't imagine that the body would not react to seven or eight hours walking every day (and carrying a 12kg pack too, don't forget!).

Whatever the reason, as the days passed and the sensation stayed with me, I was gripped by a sort of exaltation, and when, in the hills above Ascain, I saw the Atlantic Ocean for the first time, I once again raised my arms to the heavens and uttered a cry of pure joy. If only I could have remembered some appropriate verses, I would have declaimed my triumph.

I find it very difficult to describe this sensation, my words seem inadequate. Perhaps some figures would give a better idea? My walking rhythm, for example. I didn't want to force myself, my body is hardly brand new after all. In fact, whatever your age, you must learn to listen to your body even if long-distance walking forces it to go beyond its normal rhythm. You must learn to drink enough water, to rest when the body demands it, and to find the rhythm that suits it (I realised that I walk rather slowly; I measured my speed over several kilometres one day crossing the Landes, and on the flat in a straight line I don't do more than 4.7km/h, a top speed which of course is less on the slopes or at the end of the day). I don't appreciate the fast pace that some adopt, which would deprive me of that essential aspect of the pilgrimage which is to open up to your surroundings, to look at the world with new eyes. When I set out from Nevers, I found a rhythm that suited me: four hours in the morning, with a good half-hour break, an hour's pause at midday, then two to four hours in the afternoon depending on the distance, with increasingly frequent breaks according to my state of fatigue. On a good day I would cover 25km, 15km was a holiday, 30km a maximum to be exceeded only if absolutely necessary.

From Irun onwards, everything changed. The Camino del Norte has the deserved reputation of being the most arduous of the different Ways. Each day presents a succession of stiff climbs and descents, tougher than anything I had previously encountered. From Irun to San Sebastián is 25km with some 600m of ascent and descent (at times so abrupt as to need a staircase). Three days later, from Deba to Markina Xemein the distance was about the same with an ascent and descent of 700m; yet on arriving at Markina, this heady sensation of physical energy was irresistible, I had no desire to stop, and I pushed on to the Monastery of Zenarruza, 5km further and 400m higher up. I found my reward there. I had rather regretted leaving Markina Xemein behind me: the town was preparing its annual fiesta, it was full of joyful animation. But up there, in the massive monastery perched on its summit, everything was stillness, peace, balm for the soul...

I hadn't perceived the change, but one day I realised that I was walking every day for two stages of four hours each, with only a short break at midday. Still walking slowly, still lengthening and slowing the stride on the ascents, as my friend from the Alps had taught me. Eight hours walking easily took me past the 30km mark. My body had taken possession of the Way. Or perhaps rather, the Way had taken possession of me.

At Irun, everything changes. The Camino del Norte begins there, the oldest of the Caminos after the Primitivo. When pilgrims began making their way to Compostela most of the Iberian peninsula was still occupied by the Moors, and there was almost constant fighting and raiding along their northern frontier with the various Christian principalities and petty kingdoms. The road that ran along the north coast was at least partly protected by the mountains to the south, of which the Picos de Europa after Santander are only the most splendid.

The number of pilgrims changed. The Way from Vézelay is the Way of Solitude. At St Jean Pied de Port I had caught a first glimpse of the hundreds of pilgrims who head off to Spain every day. I walked alone, once again, from St Jean to Irun. From Irun to Bilbao, everything was different.

I walked no longer through the semi-deserted villages of the French countryside where sometimes you can't even find a bakery, but along a coast bustling with industry and tourism: the little port of Pasajes, Zumaya where the shipyards are still building coastal freighters, the modern seaside resort of Zarautz, Getaria where tourists and locals jostle in the bars and restaurants crowding the lanes of the old town. Supplies were no problem, I no longer needed to carry food with me since coffee, beer, and *pintxos* (the Basque equivalent of tapas) were everywhere to be found. A long black coffee, a good filling slab of tortilla, some fruit: all a man needs to set him up and keep his courage in trim.

I love the animation of Spanish towns, especially when cars, those mortal enemies of sociability, are banished from their streets. Deba, a little fishing port with a magnificent beach of fine yellow sand overlooked by imposing cliffs, was a typical case. The descent into the town nestling in its valley was even more abrupt than usual, to the point where the municipality had installed lifts to make it easier for the inhabitants of the streets higher up to access the centre. The town had grown up in a confined valley, made all the more so by the river and the railway running through it. The nature of the terrain thus imposed a certain type of architecture on the narrow streets, occupied only by a few delivery vans: buildings of four or five stories, in fine stone or prettily painted, a fine church, a little plaza. Here I settled down at a table outside one of the cafés with repeated servings of beer and *pintxos*, watching into the evening as the square gradually filled with people who sat at the tables around me to eat, to drink, to chat, until the whole town — or so it seemed to me — had gathered together in the plaza, noisy with the buzz of human voices.

I saw with delight that the peculiarly Spanish way of integrating children into social life had not been lost, not here at least. I remember a day once, on holiday on the south coast of Spain, oh a good thirty years ago, with Spanish friends. We had gone to the beach, and sat down in one of those cheap ramshackle restaurants you used to find on the beach, and which have doubtless been forbidden since by some modern regulation in the name of hygiene. The adults ate slowly, paella or *zarzuéla*, drank *vino al limón*, as the talk went round the table: it would be a long afternoon as the heat of the day wore slowly on to the warmth of a summer evening, lulled by the sound of the waves. For the children this was just boring: what they wanted was to play on the beach, paddle in the sea, build sand-castles, or play tag. Two separate worlds formed, but which split apart and came together again from time to time: an adult might get up from table to take a dip, to see that all was well with the children, to play with them no doubt; or a child might come running to show its mother a sea-shell or to explain a new game to anyone who cared to listen. And so the children had their independence, surrounded by a sensation of security; the adults could relax, while all the time ensuring an attentive presence. The adult world could welcome the children in without being invaded, the children's world was not crushed by the weight of the adults. Social life could develop at its own rhythm.

Thirty years later, in Deba's little plaza, I was enchanted to see a little troupe weaving in and out of the groups of adults, who paid it scant attention: three children, barely four years old, had appointed themselves as town band, with two toy trumpets and a plastic drum; with the utmost seriousness, they marched around the plaza, surely inhabiting a world completely of their own invention, the adult world around them becoming, for a while, evanescent and invisible.

What a contrast with those dreary industrialised landscapes, and the towns invaded by the noise and the smells of traffic! And all thanks to the valley which had prevented the town from expanding. A strange paradox, when you think about it: wherever nature imposes its rhythm on man we feel human life blossom, where man imposes his rhythm on nature we feel alienated from nature and from ourselves. Though one should be careful of facile generalisations: "man" doesn't exist in the abstract, human activity is always concretised in a particular form of social organisation, which says much about our relationships to nature and to each other in contemporary society.

Back to Irun, where the pilgrims too were very different. Until I reached St Jean, most of the people I met on the Way were more or less of my own generation; pilgrims were few, sometimes I was even alone in a hostel with seven or eight beds. But from here onwards, hostels would offer thirty, even sixty beds. Above all, almost everybody was young. It was a bit of a shock, at Irun, to find myself surrounded by people half, or even a third, my own age. A thoroughly agreeable shock, I have to say; I enjoy variety and there are few things more dismal than the separation of generations. The majority were Spanish, if I wanted to talk I would have to brush up my hesitant command of Spanish.

Memories from the *albergue* at Irun: two young Danish girls who were in front of me in the queue at the entrance, both students, one of Arabic and the other of the history of religions, because they wanted to contribute to a better understanding between peoples and cultures (but who insisted, implausibly to my mind, that Danish is not a Germanic language); a very pretty Spanish girl, so small and slim she was almost childlike, with what at first I took for black decorations on her legs, they looked very attractive on her brown skin, but they turned out to be orthopaedic supports, for this young woman suffered from a congenital weakness in her limbs but intended nonetheless to run the entire Way to Compostela; a woman from Madrid in her thirties, we walked together for a while the following day and then she left me far behind, attacking the steepest slopes as if she were on the flat; three young French lads, all of them philosophy students, who had taken their holidays to walk the Way and who I was to meet up with several times in the days that followed; and at last, a late arrival, a Scot of about my age, we ended the evening talking together and to be fair, it was good to have older people around as well.

On the first day into Spain, I caught up with the Scotsman on the Way and we descended together the steep path into Pasajes, which delighted me. It's a real little commercial, working port, its dimensions still human. There are ships and fishing boats, the narrow streets are workaday, the pilgrim walking through them feels a part of town life in its multiple dimensions. You cross the port on a little green ferry, and then you climb abruptly, straight up into the hills that dominate the river, looking down on the lighthouse as you go.

•••

Bilbao at last. I began my last day's walking from the martyred town of Guernica, victim of the Spanish Civil War. It was hot, and the weather forecast was for still more heat, and storms. I left while it was still dark, and I was already in the hills when the sun came up: a sunrise such as Turner might have painted, which enters into your spirit, into your very soul, unforgettable.

It had been worthwhile, getting up before dawn.

Later in the day, the storm broke, cleaning sky and air, dissipating the clouds as I climbed up over the final pass through the mountains.

The arrival in Bilbao was rather like the arrival in Deba, but much bigger. A modern industrial town lay spread out at my feet. The path was steep, an abrupt descent of 300m brought me to one of the old suburbs above the Casco Viejo (the old town), where a spartan little hostel awaited me. I was one of the first to arrive and for a while I simply sat alone, in the street, feeling the warm breeze on my skin as I contemplated the town below, slowly getting used to the idea that, for now, my journey was over. I had planned to spend two days in Bilbao and its museums, but I would no longer be a pilgrim. And so I prepared myself to leave this otherworldly world of the pilgrimage where I had lived for weeks — weeks so emotionally intense and filled with experience that it seemed as if months, or even years, had passed.

The *hospitalero* was a man of my own age who had lived in Bilbao all his life. He had started working in the shipyards and spoke to me of the Bilbao of yesteryear, of a town dominated by steel works, engineering, shipbuilding. Little by little, it all closed down, where once steel flowed from the forges, and ships were built by the sheer strength of men, there is now the Guggenheim Museum and its tourists. He showed me another side to the Spanish Basque Country, indeed to the whole of Spain, which I had guessed at but not seen since I left Irun: the disappearance of its industry, unemployment rising to 20%, the absence of perspective for its youth.

I told him that, somewhere between Guernica and Bilbao, I had passed the 1000km mark since my departure. Well yes, I confess: I was pleased with myself, but more than anything, astonished. It hardly seemed real. My *hospitalero* friend repeated it to a group of young girls (well, they must have been at least in their early twenties) who had just turned up and were starting their Camino at Bilbao: they opened their eyes wide, exclaimed in astonishment. Well yes, I'll say it again, why not, I'm pleased with myself: I may be "retired" but I'm not on the scrapheap yet and today I really am "*jubilado*".[6]

One thousand kilometres deserves a celebration. I made a quick detour to the little supermarket nearby, I bought wine and tapas in the hope that someone might want to share with me. I was in luck: the philosophers from Irun arrived, exhausted after losing their way crossing the last hills. They sat down at a table outside the *albergue*, we shared out food and drink, they got out their guitars, local people stopped by to chat with the *hospitalero*, other pilgrims turned up, the air was warm and pleasant, the sun sank slowly towards the opposite side of the valley, above the city. Life is good, it is still possible to hope for our battered humanity.

Thank you my friends, thanks to you I will never forget the Way that ended in Bilbao.

---

[6] In Spanish, this just means a retiree, just as *jubilación* simply means "retirement". But for a long time I assumed that it also implied someone who is "jubilant" in retirement, and I still prefer to think of it like that.

2018 — Return to Bilbao

In 2017, family obligations had forced me to break my path in Bilbao — but with the firm intention of returning and continuing to Compostela. Meanwhile, another project intervened: continuing my ongoing study of Tai Chi. For this, I spent two months in a school in China, in the town of Yangshuo (Guanxi province).[7] There I found a similar atmosphere to the one I had encountered on the Way. The students were of all ages, from all walks of life, and from all over the world (a rapid survey of my fellow students revealed that only a minority were still living in the country of their birth), united by a common goal: to understand and practice this ancient martial art. Lively discussions on all sorts of subjects bloomed and intertwined. And so I met Amaïa, a fellow student at the school and native of Bilbao. We got on very well, as we joined in discussions or went cycling together to explore the local countryside, so when I told her I intended to return to pick up the Way in Bilbao, she invited me to stay as if it were the most natural thing in the world.

My return to Bilbao thus had something special about it, and allowed me to see the town in a new light. This time I wasn't a stranger, so to speak, for Amaïa met me at the airport, welcomed me into her home, and guided me around the city.

All that seemed so natural, but when you think about it, it is

---

[7] If China or Tai Chi tempt you, you cannot do better than this traditional Tai Chi school: http://www.yangshuotaichi.com/

pretty extraordinary. An Englishman living in France, planning to visit a town in Spain, meets a native of the same town in China, on the basis of a practice born in Chinese culture. But perhaps, in the end, it's not so extraordinary after all. I prefer to believe that it's a little microcosm of a new world wide culture which is spreading step by step, a culture which will be the expression in the mind of the increasingly globalised nature of production. It's not just goods that move from one continent to another. Ideas do too, and even people despite the suspicions of governments and the frontiers that are put in their way.

All this gave me much to think about, though I confess I've not arrived at any conclusions. Amaïa is not just Basque, she's a *bilbaína*. She loves her city and her language's survival means a lot to her (although she had to learn it as an adult, since she was born when speaking Basque was still banned by the Franco regime). But I'll come back to the question of language later, because first I want to tell you something about the city.

I first saw Bilbao when I was 18 years old, accompanying my father on one of his study trips to the Maghreb. We had taken the ferry from Plymouth to Bilbao, before crossing Spain to take the ferry again at Algeciras. That was in 1970. My memory of the town is above all one of blackness: the weather grey and cloudy, buildings blackened by smoke and pollution, the streets busy with people who seemed to bear the scars of hard industrial labour, doubtless also of their memories of the Civil War and the ferocious repression meted out by Franco to the workers in general and the Basques in particular, for which the bombardment of Guernica, immortalised by Picasso, remains a lasting symbol. With hindsight, my memories of Bilbao are mingled with those of a childhood visit to my grandfather's family in Tow Law in the North of England, one of those towns whose only reason for existence was the mines around which it had grown up. There too, the streets, the people, everything in fact, seemed to be blackened by coal dust and industrial dirt.

Bilbao was like that because of the exceptionally high-grade iron ore to be found further inland, and which was already mined by the Romans. Thanks to its iron ore, Bilbao became an industrial town, the river flowing to the Atlantic lined with steelworks and shipyards. Now all that has pretty much disappeared, with the same results that are to be seen in all the old steel regions in Europe and the United States: endemic unemployment, and devastated urban landscapes.

And then, the city reinvented itself. We went for a walk in a park high above the city, from where we could see the whole course of the river: the Casco Viejo, the old quarter which today is filled with the bustle of bars, restaurants, music; the fish market, which still sells fish but has also made room for the overflow from the Casco Viejo; then the promenade along the river bank leading to the Guggenheim Museum, the centrepiece of the city's cultural district; then the opera house, an enormous building whose walls are all in rusted steel as a reminder of the steelworks of yore. Further on, we could see more abandoned industrial areas awaiting renovation, and further still towards Portugalete there is the Rialia, a fine little museum devoted to industrial history and art.

All that I could see with my own eyes, but thanks to Amaïa I was able to see deeper. She told me how her grandfather had been a fisherman, and how the fishing boats on their return from the sea used to race up the river to be the first to land their catch at the market, and so command the best price. Today of course, the fishing is largely industrialised, but they still race the old boats. I saw one in training a few days later at Castro Urdiales, and it reminded me of the gig racing practiced to this day in the Scilly Isles off the coast of Cornwall.

I was dubious about the opera, which seemed to me an indulgence of the wealthy rather an a rejuvenation of the city as a whole. But Amaïa told me that every year the opera puts on a programme over several days where the tickets are sold at prices within the reach of all but the very poorest.

Let's begin our visit with the Casco Viejo, where I had stayed the previous year after my first night in the *albergue*, in a thoroughly agreeable backpacker's hostel. The old quarter seduced me immediately. I loved the busy constricted streets, whence cars are banned so that human life can find expression. Sheltered from the sun in summer, and from the worst of the winds off the ocean in winter, nothing is standardised, everything looks somewhat anarchic, or perhaps it would be more exact to say "organic". I find the style of its buildings very attractive, often with balconies sheltered behind windows from floor to ceiling, a necessary precaution in this northern coastal climate which can often be cold and rainy.

In the Casco Viejo there are all kinds of bars, cafés, restaurants, and little shops of the kind which disappeared long ago everywhere else. Look at this shop for example, whose sign announces *Bacalao y productos coloniales* ("Cod and colonial produce") and which seems given over almost entirely to salted cod and olive oil. What contradictions we find, yet again, in our modern world! Bilbao is an example, on a larger scale and very successful, of a phenomenon which I have seen over and over again on the Way: a "historical" town centre, where money has been spent to restore, to pedestrianise, and here it works. People come, either tourists or locals, because this is where it's most agreeable to drink, to eat out, to stroll about. The outskirts are full of industrial zones and trading estates each one uglier than its neighbour, and long, desperately straight, streets of ugly concrete apartment blocks, where the shops are either shut or never even opened and where very often, as one can readily guess, people don't have the means to offer themselves an evening out in the centre. As a traveller, you end up living in a sort of simulacrum of a human town, where the inhabitants cannot live, except perhaps a small minority.

But enough of these gloomy reflections! For the moment the

weather is fine, I'm back in Bilbao which I love, and I'm in good company. You must also let yourself live, let yourself go in the enjoyment of strolling through the streets, stopping for a drink, hearing the constant echo of voices (for the Basques are Spanish enough to talk in the streets, a lot, and loudly). I need to return again to taste this very special town to the full.

The Casco Viejo spreads out across both banks of the river, and walking along the riverside you come to the Guggenheim Museum, whose construction on an old industrial site kicked off the city's regeneration.

Outside the museum is an exhibition of photographs showing the evolution of the city and the river, from the first shipyards which were barely more than makeshift workshops set up around a few sailing ships hauled up on the riverbank, to the 20th century factories with their gigantic cranes and all the paraphernalia of heavy industry. Amaïa told me that before the museum was built, the site was so full of old containers and other industrial rubbish that she found it hard to imagine where they would find the space to put it.

And when she first heard of the Guggenheim project, she wondered what could be the point of it: nobody ever came to visit Bilbao!

I had never realised before (which shows a lack of imagination on my part) just how fraught the city's regeneration had been at the time. It must have been an extraordinary change to live through. Once Bilbao had been filled right to its heart with the noise, the smells, the harsh sounds, of industrial life; people built, they manufactured, and no doubt there was a certain pride in knowing that they had supplied the whole world with steel, and that the ships they had built furrowed the world's oceans. Then everything was dismantled or fell into abandon leaving nothing but ruins and the desperate sensation that all the bitter struggles against redundancies had been for nothing, that the world had changed and there was nothing to be done about it.

Today the strange forms of the Guggenheim, adorned with burnished steel in homage to the city's industrial past, loom along the riverbank. The museum is the centrepiece of a whole cultural district which is still under construction on the riverbanks running down towards the sea. Apparently the Guggenheim and all the associated touristic activity employs 47,000 people and contributes more than €2 billion every year to the budget of the Spanish *Pais Vasco* (the Basque region). I ponder, not for the first time, this strange phenomenon (of which I am a part of course) which pushes people to "go and see" with their own eyes. It can't be completely new: surely in antiquity, travellers went to see the "Seven wonders of the world", among them the Colossus of Rhodes or the lighthouse of Alexandria? What is it that pushes us to do that, or that drives people out on the Way? Perhaps I'll have more to say on the subject later, when my ideas are a bit clearer: after all, it's one of my pilgrimage's aims, to get my ideas straight…

But for the moment, I want to talk about the Guggenheim itself, above all about its architecture rather than the collection, which is a fine one by all means, but if you're a Parisian like me, not much different from what you can see any day at the Orsay, the Orangerie, or Beaubourg.

With one exception. By far the most interesting part of the collection to my mind is the work of Richard Serra, an American sculptor whose work I discovered with enthusiasm. Serra specialises in monumental works constructed of steel plates, and a 25-year contract with the Guggenheim has given him the space and the time to spread himself.

I came to his work from above, looking down from a balcony the whole length of the large hall where his installations are on display. It seemed at first almost childishly simple. The construction materials are 20-ton plates of raw steel, arranged in rounded interconnecting forms that seem to create a series of labyrinths. I confess that I was dubious at first. It seems to me that there is a tendency, when one has nothing to say, to say it very loud, or in works of art, very big; a tendency to crush all criticism or resistance under the sheer size of the work, like those colossal statues of the Egyptian Pharaohs. To tell the truth, I'm inclined to find such stuff pretentious more than anything. But as I descended into the exhibition and walked round and through Serra's work, I fell under the spell. Seen close up, the steel which had seemed dull and flat at a distance revealed colours of a strange and seductive subtlety, changing and shifting as I shifted position. As I walked through a sculpture the spaces created between the plates changed also, imperceptibly. I had the sensation of being caught in a three-dimensional illusion: intellectually, I knew that the space I walked in towards the centre of the piece must be closing in on me, and yet it seemed on the contrary to be opening out. It was disconcerting, unsettling, almost frightening even.

I came out of the exhibition impressed and excited, even more so once I had watched the interview with Serra that is projected next to the sculpture, and where he explained how he had come to use such an unusual raw material. His father had worked in the shipyards and Serra had known them well in his childhood; what then could be more natural for him than to return to this childhood matter, steeped in the affects of the relationship between father and son? And what better sculptor could there be, to embody the city's transition away from its industrial past?

Strangely — and that brings me back to the museum's architecture — although Serra is a friend of the architect Frank Gehry, he didn't seem to appreciate particularly the Guggenheim, which he described as "architectonically false" (don't ask me exactly what he meant by that!); he was especially critical of a general tendency to conflate sculpture and architecture, which for him should remain two distinct disciplines, with different purposes.

Now, I'm instinctively in favour of architecture that gets out of the rut and is ready to take risks (as my painter friend says, you can't create art without taking risks), and there are few things more soul-destroying than the endless banality of modern building which is in neither good nor bad taste, but simply without any kind of taste at all. This was my initial state of mind when I first went to see Gehry's Louis Vuitton building in Paris, a strange edifice which is supposed to look like a yacht, all sails set. But I was disillusioned by its interior, and ended up agreeing with a friend who had arrived at the same conclusion as Serra: a building (unlike a sculpture) has first and foremost a function, and must be faithful to that function; it must be judged on the basis of the relationship between the interior and the exterior, and of the movement from one to the other, by the geometry of its interior space. Everything depends on this, and at this level the Vuitton building is not a success.

What about the Bilbao Guggenheim? Here, I find myself much less categorical. The first time I saw it, I found the outside more interesting and the interior space more interesting and convincing, so to speak, than the Vuitton. But in discussing it with Amaïa, who is an unconditional fan of the Guggenheim, I realised that there is a whole other dimension to the building. Its purpose is not just to display works of art, but to be itself an affirmation of the living city, of its past and its ambition. It's as if the spirit of two towns passed, how consciously or not I've no idea, through Gehry, to take concrete form in the two buildings. From this angle, the difference between the two is perfectly understandable. Bilbao is a working, industrial city, its past is made of hard labour and suffering, of steel and ships, here it declares its determination to survive, and to live. I know very well that a city, like a country, is made of different social classes with different and conflicting interests, but nonetheless, I think it is possible to feel the soul of a city made up of all those intersecting human lives and histories, whose roots and setting it has been…

What could the Vuitton building express? Nothing but the town of Neuilly-sur-Seine, flaunting its riches between Paris' wealthy 16th Arrondissement and the financial district of La Défense. A town personified by its one-time mayor Nicolas Sarkozy, master of bling and the superficiality of the *nouveau riche*. Decidedly, Neuilly will never be Bilbao.

Later on the Way, I talked over the Guggenheim with a German architect who had not liked it either, for all the reasons I've just mentioned: the form does not correspond to the function. I very quickly guessed (correctly as it turned out) that she was a fan of Bauhaus, a movement that was both architectural and artistic, and even in part social and revolutionary, which wanted to conceive not just how buildings should look but how they should be lived in. Like Bauhaus, she liked pure and simple lines, stripped of any spirit of fantasy.

This bothered me, and once again I was brought up short by my own ambivalence. On the one hand I agreed with her, I too like and admire Bauhaus buildings. But would I want to live in them? In general, if you gave people a choice, would they want to live in a habitat all made of straight lines? There's no gainsaying, that the majority have no choice but to live in great apartment blocks made of desperately straight lines in every direction. When I remember my own reactions towards the Casco Viejo, or a town like Siena in Italy, or indeed my own home town of Oxford, I can't help thinking that we humans are more organically inclined, and that we need a habitat that changes and adapts, that we can adapt ourselves, and that is integrated with the world of plants...

My mind wandered off into a fantasy about a new kind of architecture... That bridge in Amsterdam built by 3D printers excited me, for example. The forms, calculated by computer to use materials as sparingly as possible, seemed closer to the natural forms of plants than to the traditions of the building trade. I began to wonder about the possibilities that bio-tech might open up. Could we imagine genetically modified trees which would grow in such a way as to create living-spaces in their interior, which would create a truly living building, and which might live in symbiosis with decorative plants, perhaps with plants whose chlorophyll would generate electricity or purify grey water? So we would truly live "in nature", surrounded not by aggressive rectilinear shapes of concrete, but by natural forms, with their strange and unexpected curves and contours, surrounded also by the warm colours of polished wood which would never need to be painted but would maintain itself thanks to its own essential oils, in the manner of the *lignum vitae*.

Perhaps it's time to stop, before delirium sets in, and I take off into a world of science fiction…

Such were my thoughts, inspired by my visit to the Guggenheim and the contradictory opinions I heard about it. But I cannot leave Bilbao without saying something as well about the city's Museum of Fine Arts (Museo de Bellas Artes), whose collection is very fine, and even, perhaps, more interesting than the Guggenheim's. This is above all due, at least in my eyes, to its collection of works by modern Basque artists, of whom I had never heard before. Here, everything Amaïa had to say about language was brought forcefully home to me: every language has its own idiom, expresses a different perspective on the world surrounding us. Not better necessarily, nor worse either, but different. It is clear that all these Basque artists were active in the international artistic movements of their day, but in their own idiom, from a viewpoint which was not entirely the same as that of their better-known French contemporaries, for example. We know Gauguin of course, but not Francisco Durrio (sculptor, ceramist, and goldsmith) who worked with him, and introduced his work to Spain. In Durrio's work, clearly, we can see Gauguin's influence, or perhaps a shared sensibility, but filtered through a different imagination nurtured in Durrio's own culture.

More directly, we see reflected in the work of Joaquin Sorolla, the harsh and difficult lives of Basque fishermen. And so an art shaped by the expressive modes of its time can translate for others the experience of a particular way of life. Bio-diversity is as necessary for human culture as it is for the rest of the living world.

I left feeling that to visit Bilbao without taking in the Museum of Fine Arts would mean missing something of the city's very soul.

There would be more to say, much more no doubt. But the Way is calling me again, with its stories to live and to tell. Perhaps one day, I will return…

I sacrifice to convention

My original intention had been to avoid the conventional travelogue and to give an account of my thoughts day by day, as they were prompted by the landscapes I passed through and the people I met. But too often I found the energy lacking after 8-10 hours walking, and so it's only in Lugo, where I stopped for two days, that I found myself able to take the time, and to look back over the paths I had taken. And despite all my best intentions, custom does demand that the writer should give some account of his physical as well as his mental wanderings.

Back then to Bilbao, on the point of leaving the city by the Camino del Norte which runs along the north coast of Spain. I didn't intend to follow the Norte all the way, but to turn off towards Oviedo and the Camino Primitivo, partly to see Oviedo and partly because the Primitivo passes over the mountains, which I love even more than the sea.

Much later, on the Way, I had a strange experience. A fellow pilgrim asked me how long I had been walking (a common enough subject of conversation on the Way). I pondered for a while… I realised that I was incapable of answering: ten days perhaps? or maybe twelve? I pulled out my *credential* (the pilgrim's passport, where every day is marked by the stamp of the hostel where you stayed): I realised that I had been walking for twenty days, that time had lost all meaning, and that my passage had left only fugitive, disordered memories.

To return to my starting point, I have to say that I had envisaged the road out of Bilbao with some trepidation. Towns generally have a talent for surrounding even the most beautiful historic centre with unbelievable quantities of ugliness: apartment blocks that look like barracks (or prisons), supermarkets, interminable suburbs of little houses without the slightest individuality of character, factory outlets, warehouses, industrial and trading estates, in short all the clutter which apparently is so indispensable to the modern economy that it can impose its ugly cheap architecture without encountering the least resistance. Tarmac under your feet, and only unsightly landscapes to admire are a drain on your vital energy as the kilometres go by.

But in the end, it wasn't too bad. The Way leaves the city centre along Autonomía, a long and quite attractive avenue full of shops, and then climbs abruptly into the woods where the land is too steep to build on. Once in the heights, you walk through woods and villages, with a splendid view over the city and the river spread out almost beneath your feet. True, the murmur you hear comes from the motorway rather than the sea, but on the whole the walk is pleasant enough. At one point your feet even tread the original medieval stone pilgrims' road, lost now far from the city's bustle. Then, you descend into the peaceful suburb of Barakaldo where the streets are busy, there are bars and groceries full of cherries in this season, a fruit I can never resist (I didn't even try, preferring to follow Oscar Wilde's precept that the only way to deal with temptation is to give in), and shortly after you arrive in Portugalete.

I have a soft spot for Portugalete. I like the narrow streets of the old quarter that run down towards the river, which is close enough to the sea to be navigable even for large ships. Shipping on the river was once important enough to prompt the construction there of a transporter bridge, which today is one of the very rare examples of this unusual technology still in activity. Passengers and vehicles cross the river in a sort of gondola suspended below the upper part of the bridge. I had taken it in 2017, and had found it a strange sensation, crossing the river at the height of a ship's deck, but suspended in the air above the water.

The Way out of Portugalete is not particularly attractive, but it is rendered a good deal less disagreeable than it would otherwise have been, by the pedestrian and cycle tracks that pass safely over and beside the inevitable roads and motorways. After a while, this track leaves the roads behind, and follows its own way through the countryside and villages, before dropping down through a long valley full of trees and flowers, to the coast, from whence the way follows the shore more or less all the way to Castro Urdiales. Castro is not bad. Once you've made your way through the apartment blocks of the seaside resort, you arrive at an old port overlooked by an impressive church and the old fortress.

Amaïa had told me that even though they don't use the old rowing boats of her grandfather's day to go fishing, they still race them. Apparently the Castro team is one of the best, and I had the good fortune to spot them off the jetty during their sea training. The sea was calm enough that day, and yet the boat seemed to disappear between the waves. I wondered how the rowers managed to keep their oars biting in the water. What a life it must have been, when every thing like that depended on sheer physical strength…

I had an encounter on the Way into Laredo, that touched me. Just before arriving in the town, the Way is poorly signed and I left the other pilgrims behind me on the main road, dropping down into a steep valley. I found myself in a small village, wondering which way to go, just in front of a pretty house. The family was sitting round the table out front, eating their midday meal (well, their two o'clock meal; this was Spain after all). They offered me water, invited me to sit down, offered me tortilla, bread, fruit. The young daughter of the house spoke English remarkably well. All this done with such kindness and simplicity, that I walked on lightheartedly, optimistic anew as to the prospects for the human species.

In Laredo I stayed in the convent in the old town, so on the day of my arrival I saw nothing of the seaside resort. The following morning began with a stretch of several kilometres along the sea front, past Laredo's interminable seaside apartments, which seemed intended to confirm that the more beautiful the beach, the uglier are the buildings put up next to it. But there was a happy compensation. Once you get to the end, you have to take a ferry to cross the estuary. On the Laredo side, there is only the beach where the ferry lets down a simple plank for you to board. In ones and twos, pilgrims arrived and spread themselves around on the sand, admiring the sunrise and the calm of the sea. From the other side, Laredo and its apartment blocks were lost in the mist, nothing remained but the sea, the sky, the sand, and the little ferry.

But then my courage left me, bit by bit. There are days like that, you feel disillusioned with everything and you end up wondering what you're doing on this interminable tarmac of the Way wending its way through a countryside full of empty holiday homes and lifeless villages without so much as a bar. At long last I left the coast, once again the Way ran through green fields and woods. Finally at day's end, I arrived in the huge (100 beds) *albergue* of Guëmes, still in a foul mood, and none too pleased to be told that before eating I would have to listen to an explanation of the *albergue's* philosophy; I couldn't help grumbling to myself that at least when you stay in a hotel, the manager doesn't feel he has the right to tell you everything he thinks about life, so you can judge for yourselves the kind of temper I was in.

Still, I really must tell you about the *albergue* at Guëmes, because it has become something of a legend along the Camino del Norte, as I found out later from other pilgrims. And to be fair, once I was showered and rested, and had taken the time to enjoy the well-kept gardens around the building, I was much more disposed to listen to a philosophy lecture.

Which was just as well, because it was interesting. The *albergue* was still run by Ernesto, 80 years old, with a patriarchal white beard and a definite charisma. Not only that, the *albergue* is his birthplace; he and his family had been forced to leave when he was still a child, to escape from the poverty and hunger of the countryside and seek work in Catalonia. He had entered holy orders, and after twelve years studying philosophy and theology, he had been posted to an isolated parish high in the mountains. There — as he put it — philosophy and theology were of little help to him, the life was one of hard labour, but also of solidarity, mutual assistance, and a concern for others. And so he, from a peasant family himself, had learned from the peasants. And today, he was trying to live this lesson of life, and to spread his vision of general solidarity throughout the Way. And although I don't share his faith, how well I can understand his desire to act in solidarity with others. Indeed, is not this feeling very common, that solidarity is missing in the modern world? And that it is even one of the main things we are lacking in life?

Ernesto told us that, that evening, we were 67 pilgrims of 17 different nationalities. Not for the first time, nor the last, I wondered what effect this might have in the long term, these minglings of people who manage, despite the obstacles of language and culture, to communicate something shared in common.

After Guëmes you can follow the road into Somo, but it's much more agreeable to take the longer route over the cliffs and the beach. At Somo itself, you take another ferry to cross the estuary into Santander.

I should probably give Santander another chance, but on the face of it the city didn't speak to me. I didn't feel it as vibrant as Bilbao. The seafront seen from the ferry proclaimed the city's wealth, the beggars in its tree-lined avenues bespoke its poverty, the Way out of the city was a concentrate of everything I dislike (and on top of that it was raining), and frankly, gentle reader, I wouldn't blame you if you were to take the train, and even to take it for several stations to avoid the endless suburb of little houses that I for one generally find utterly depressing. For myself, I was seized with a fit of obstinacy that kept me walking to the village of Boo de Peliagos and its welcoming *albergue*.

Here, I can't resist a pleasing story. Boo is on the banks of a river that you have to cross before you can continue on to Santillana del Mar (oddly named, since it is nowhere near the sea). The Way is thus forced to make a detour of 9km through tedious suburbs, just to get to the first bridge across the river. It's frustrating, because there is a bridge at Boo, but it is reserved for the railway and so forbidden to pilgrims and other such pedestrian animals. The solution is to catch the train at Boo and get off at the station on the other side, a solution entirely justified in my eyes by the fact that, in the Middle Ages, there was a ferry which carried pilgrims across the river for free.

After looking at the map, I decided that the good of my soul did not demand that I walk all round the substantial chemical plant further on along the Way, so I shortened the day considerably by taking the train as far as Barredo. Following which, an easy and pleasant 12km took me into Santillana.

In the book where he recounts his experience of the Way, Jean-Christophe Rufin clearly doesn't think much of Santillana because of its status as a tourist trap, and I can understand his feelings. But I think he oversimplifies the issues, and it's a question I feel I will have to come back to later. Let's just say that Santillana, which claims to be one of Spain's most beautiful villages, made me think of Gargilesse on the Way from Vézelay, where I had passed through the previous year: both are almost too beautiful. At least the streets of Santillana, unlike those of Gargilesse, are lively with herds of tourists ambling peaceably through the town; with just a little imagination you could transform them into herds of cows and so escape back in time to an earlier epoch.

I had planned to spend two nights in Santillana, to give me time to make the detour to the caves of Altamira and their prehistoric art. I had the good fortune to find lodgings in a religious *albergue*, "Il Convento", in what had once been a monastery. The building is beautiful, surrounded by a fine garden which I was unable to enjoy to the full because of the rain. But I did get to sleep in a monk's cell; these, being small of course, only fitted two beds, and I had the rare privilege of sleeping alone for two nights.

And then, Santillana intrigued me. I can't help thinking that its history must be unusual for the village to boast so many fine old stone houses, which must surely have belonged to the aristocracy, or at least to the well-to-do. What were they all doing there? Perhaps they had gathered round the collegiate church dedicated to St Juliana of Nicomedia, built in the 12th century, and which is well worth the visit. Religious architecture in Spain has a predilection for the Romanesque and seems to have avoided the gothic style entirely; this church has preserved the purity of the original structure, and largely avoided the overbearing Baroque woodwork of later centuries. The cloisters are very fine, their proportions discreet, and the columns decorated with allegorical motifs which I found reminiscent of the Norman church of Monreale in Sicily, though more forbidding and austere.

I will spare you the details of the tortures inflicted by her own father on poor St Juliana before her martyrdom, which are recounted at length on a notice in the church. Doubtless the Catholic devotee would be horrified (I imagine that that is precisely the point), but I couldn't help thinking that they sounded remarkably like the torments undergone by the victims of the Holy Inquisition. The Catholic Church has a remarkable ability to reinvent itself, to shrug off the horrors of its past (and of which the Inquisition was only the most visible and the most outrageous) and to present itself in a new skin, like a snake. The same church whose Pope today puts himself forward (quite sincerely I don't doubt) as a defender of the poor, very nearly excommunicated St Francis for having preached the poverty of Christ. Strange too, that several Catholics I met along the Way seemed to consider the Church's temporal structure as entirely secondary, when Catholic doctrine insists that the faithful cannot approach God without the intercession of the Church. But all that is too complicated for me to deal with here… Suffice it to say that the Church and its beliefs seem to me full of impossible contradictions.

After Santillana, you leave behind you, more or less, the disagreeable industrial areas that you find between Bilbao and Santander. Just as well, I was beginning to feel I had had enough of them. Perhaps my irritation also had something to do with the weather which had remained obstinately gloomy and dull, especially in the afternoon.

The countryside after Santillana is more attractive, the Way keeps more to the footpaths and away from the roads, and then you arrive at the charming town of Comillas where the municipal *albergue* is established in the old prison (follow the signs to "El Carcel"!). It's well worth getting to Comillas in time to visit the villa "El Capricho" (the Caprice); it was one of the first commissions of the architect Antonio Gaudi, who was only 26 when he drew up the plans. El Capricho offers us an insight not just into Gaudi's career, but into the social history of the region, for the house was built for an "*Indiano*". Just as the British continue to call the Caribbean islands "the West Indies", so in 19th century Spain, the Americas were called "*los Indios*", and many were the inhabitants of this poverty-stricken region who fled to "the Indies" in the hopes of making their fortunes. Some of them succeeded, so well indeed that they were able to return home and build themselves sumptuous houses where they could show off their riches to their countrymen. I imagine they did so with all the more pleasure in that they had sailed away poor, and returned wealthier than those who had once looked down on them. All along the coast, especially in Comillas and Llanes, you come across houses built in a colonial style that is eccentric but not displeasing, sometimes handsomely restored, but sometimes abandoned and in ruins; the family must have fallen on hard times, or maybe it didn't come through the Civil War unscathed. The "*Indianos*", it should be said, certainly didn't get rich by themselves, they only did so by exploiting the labour of Indians and slaves.

One oddity of the returnees, they seem to have wanted absolutely to be ennobled with the most splendid titles possible. It's said that Spain is the most royalist country in the world because every Spaniard thinks he is king. I don't know if that's true, but I was struck by the number of even quite modest houses bearing the family coat of arms on the wall facing the street. In Comillas, one local boy at least not only made good but became extremely rich and a friend of the king to boot, who made him a Marquis. A well-known architect of the day (Joan Martorell) built him an overblown vaguely Gothic monstrosity just outside the town (it was closed the day I was there). Gaudi's house was designed, not for the Marquis but for his lawyer who, being a bachelor, only needed a modest residence (well, relatively modest). He was a well-educated man, a musician who also took an interest in botany and biology, and Gaudi decorated the house with appropriate motifs. The balcony balustrades are formed like musical notations, the doors and windows are surrounded with ceramic flowers imported at great expense and with great difficulty — given the primitive transport of the day — from far-away Barcelona.

Leaving Comillas early in the morning, I was rewarded by a glorious sun filling the air with light.

Here, the Way runs right along the beach, for several kilometres. I think I must have been the only person to have walked it that day, apart from the dog whose tracks intercepted my footsteps. I was completely alone, the silence was broken only by the lapping of the waves. Transcendance was surely there, somewhere, just the other side of the horizon perhaps.

I had wanted to stop at Colombres to see the museum devoted to the history of the *Indianos*, but the *albergue* was full so I walked on to Buelna, where there is nothing much except the *albergue*, agreeable enough. That made a long day, but repaid by dreamlike views over the cliffs and the ocean.

After Buelna, it was only a short day into Llanes, a very attractive little harbour town. It boasts a remarkable number of fine colonial style houses, both ruined and restored, the town itself is peaceful and relaxed around its fishing port. Just as in Deba, the municipal *albergue* has taken over the railway station, and is agreeably spacious.

In Llanes I tasted Asturian cider for the first time. It is more acidic than cider in England, still and rougher on the tongue. According to the locals, the proper way to drink it is as follows: pour a small quantity into a pint glass while holding the bottle as high as possible, to aerate the cider; then knock it back in one gulp. In principle the waiter should do it for you (the pouring, not the gulping), and show off his art. But if the waiter doesn't know how then technology will come to your aid by means of an electronic device in which you fit the bottle and the glass; press the button to get good dose of cider, properly aerated!

The days that followed, I suffered the consequences of the kind of miscalculation I sometimes commit. It all began because I wanted to do a short day's walk into Oviedo, to give myself time to visit the town without having to stay a second night. It was forecast to rain, and there are few things more aggravating than to spend time in a town where you don't have a place of your own to get out of the rain (all the more because the *albergue peregrino* in Oviedo, although otherwise perfectly agreeable and correct, is housed in a thoroughly lugubrious building, which looks far more like a prison than El Carcel at Comillas). So I calculated my distances backwards from Oviedo, and ended up — I won't bore you with the details — walking from Ribadesella to Pola da Siero in two days, that is to say 70km with a lot of up and down, including one day of 40km which pushed me to the limits of my endurance. And I regretted having pressed on to Villaviciosa rather than stopping in the pretty little *albergue* at Priesca. But there are no shops anywhere near Priesca and you have to do your own cooking, there was nothing to eat in my pack, and so on. Still, the *albergue* in Pola was a compensation. Pola itself is an uninteresting town, with the exception of the *albergue*, an attractive religious building all newly done up and surrounded by a fine garden. Better still, just opposite the entrance is a bar whose sympathetic vibrations I could feel as soon as I walked through the door, where you eat well, and which fills with animated conversation as the evening wears on. Not for the first, nor the last time, I wondered about this sensitivity I seem to have (and which I suppose we all share) to a place's atmosphere; how much is it part of the place itself, how much is it merely a product of my own subjectivity? At all events, it seems to me that the further along the Way I go, the more sensitive I become to the "feeling" of a place, as soon as I enter it. I know almost immediately whether I will feel at ease there or not, and I rarely seem to make a mistake. I can't find a better expression for this feeling than that old word from the 1960s, the "vibrations". Maybe I'm growing antennae.

In the bar at Pola I met a gay couple from New Zealand; they were a couple of handsome, strapping young lads, and we made friends straight away. The following day, I left early for Oviedo under a sky that alternated between gloomy and positively wet. A couple of hours into the Way, my two friends from the night before caught me up, striding along at a good pace. I was touched when they slowed down so that we could talk along the Way, and walk into Oviedo together. So I learnt that Todd was an actor, and Kip an actor when he had to, but a theatre producer by taste. I think it's the first time that I have had a chance to talk to professional actors (though I do remember, as a child, having been much impressed to meet the real Catwoman, or rather the actress who played the part in the original Batman TV series), and to get an impression of how they lived. It seemed to me that it must be terribly disconcerting to have to get under the skin of a character, to take his life story and his emotions for one's own. And then, what a difference between the theatre and the cinema, or the television! In the theatre at least, a play unfolds in its chronological order and the actor can flow with the story. Whereas in film, each scene is treated quite separately. One scene might last only a few seconds, and is not necessarily filmed in order to boot. How is it possible to adapt the voice, the face, the stance, to become a different person at the flick of a switch, so to speak?

I was fascinated by Kip's description of a theatre piece that he had co-authored and produced, based on the story of the Apollo 13 mission, which should have landed on the moon, but almost ended in disaster when a technical fault in the capsule forced the astronauts to return as fast as possible before their oxygen ran out. The tale has already been made into an excellent film (*Apollo 13*, with Tom Hanks), but in this theatre production, the aim was to get the audience to take part.[8] The auditorium was converted into a mock-up of the Apollo mission control room in Houston, and each spectator on arriving was led, not to an ordinary theatre stall, but to a console equipped with screens, indicators, switches, in short, invited to play the part of a mission control team member. So the play became a collective, interactive, and largely improvised work, which must have demanded a great deal of ingenuity from the actors who had to play the control room managers, while at the same time organising the audience.

---

[8] The interested reader can find a detailed account on the play's web site: https://www.apollo13live.com/about

As expected, it was raining as we walked into Oviedo, but it was our good fortune to arrive on a Sunday. The cathedral was open (which is rare in Spain), for Mass of course, and we made our way inside — after all, what would the world be coming to if pilgrims on St James' Way weren't allowed in to hear Mass? The church was packed tight, and the choir very fine, a pure feminine voice rising into the far-off heights of the nave. Even wet and weary as we were, how could we not be moved?

An oddity of the town, on Sundays it fills up with people in traditional Asturian costume who stroll through the streets playing music. I was very surprised, even more so when the tourist office informed me that this had not been put on for some special occasion, but was simply a normal Sunday pastime, for pleasure and amusement. In a street full of *sidrerías* (that is, bars and restaurants specialising in cider) strolling musicians would stop in front of a bar and, for the price of a few beers offered by the establishment, play to attract customers. Woody Allen, apparently, was so vocal in his praise of Oviedo that there is a statue of him somewhere in the town; I can perfectly understand his feelings.

Oviedo marks the beginning of the Camino Primitivo. According to legend, this was where Alfonso II began his pilgrimage to verify the authenticity of the saintly remains that had just been discovered at Compostela. The Way becomes steeper, then at Salas you get a real foretaste of the climbs for which the Primitivo is renowned. The landscapes are magnificent, even with the cloudy and sometimes wet weather; they reminded me of the Marches between England and Wales, in the counties of Powys and Herefordshire, which I always felt were some of the most beautiful in the British Isles.

One of the pleasures of the Primitivo (let's be honest) is the respect you get from pilgrims who arrive in Compostela by the Camino Francés and who at most have had a light upward stroll over the Pyrenees to contend with. When they learn that you have come from the Norte and still more from the Primitivo, their eyes open wide and this is the moment for you to smile modestly and say that no, it really wasn't that bad. And really, it isn't. The Primitivo is called "the knee breaker" but that seems to me a gross exaggeration. Certainly, there are some upward stretches which tend to be a bit long and a bit steep, followed inevitably by downward stretches which tend to be a bit steep and a bit long. Certainly, too, I would hesitate to go straight at it without any prior training (two weeks of the Norte is excellent training). But just slow your pace on the ascents and take care on the descents, and there is no reason to deprive yourself of landscapes which are never less than beautiful and sometimes verge on the sublime.

For reasons I've forgotten, but which seemed convincing at the time, I decided to spread out my days in such a way as to spend the night in smaller *albergues*. This is how I ended up in Escamplero, Doriga, and Bodenaya, and I can recommend all three. At Esclampero you get the keys to the *albergue* from a nearby bar-cum-restaurant, a welcoming hostelry where I ate very well that evening. Doriga turned out to be barely more than a hamlet clustered round a pretty church. The rain had transformed the path into Doriga into a veritable mud-bath, and it led me to a sort of bar, grocery and restaurant all rolled into one, with a wooden shed at the bottom of the garden for pilgrims to sleep in. The regulars at the bar welcomed me into local life, but with just one problem: my hesitant Spanish was apparently so convincing that everyone spoke as if I was fluent and understood everything, with the result that I ended up understanding next to nothing.

You arrive at Bodenaya after a climb of several kilometres out of Salas, where every time I said to myself that it couldn't get any steeper, it did. My only regret came later, when I learned that I had missed an excellent museum of old manuscripts at Salas; I had only stopped there long enough to eat a tortilla. But I didn't regret the *albergue* at Bodenaya, which is really worth the stay if only for the kindness of the *hospitaleros* David and Celia. The pilgrims trickled in soaked, their boots covered in mud, exhausted by the long ascent. We were welcomed with simplicity and generosity, and the next morning woke to find our boots cleaned and our clothes washed and folded, arranged like presents under the Christmas tree. The *albergue* is housed in a small old building, the floors and roof supported by ancient wood beams, and the walls covered with testimonies from previous pilgrims of the welcome they had received. Flags, often, and the scarves of football teams. Now usually, I am completely allergic to national flags, detestable symbols of national pride responsible for so much bloodshed, but I was touched despite that. For I have no doubt that the pilgrims who sent their flags to decorate the wall did so simply to bear witness to their origins, and to their desire to contribute to fraternal whole that we want the Way to be. I was reminded of the revolutionary Russian poet Vladimir Maïakovski and his unfulfilled dream, where every nation on Earth would come together to contribute its own specific qualities to the new united humanity where the nation would no longer exist, or at least would no longer be synonymous with blood and exclusion. He had hoped to see such a humanity born out of the October Revolution, history knows how tragically he was disappointed.

Our *hospitaleros* were great believers in the "spirit of the Way", which they hoped would unite all pilgrims in one great family of solidarity and mutual assistance. I couldn't help remarking to David that a lot of families hardly live up to that ideal, but in fact I came to realise that very often people use the family as a symbol for affectionate relationships and solidarity, simply because that is our principal reference point for such sentiments to find expression.

The meal was prepared and eaten in common. I'm often reticent about joining in a shared meal, since the feelings it is supposed to express and evoke can sometimes feel rather forced; but at Bodenaya, everything is done with such simplicity and is so freely given that it would be a shame, and churlish indeed, not to take part. How many different nationalities sat together round the table? I forget: Germans, British (which is unusual), French, Swedish, Dutch, Belgian, Korean, American. There is something about sharing food which melts away differences, and reunites us with our common ancestral humanity, and I can never help being moved by such moments.

At table, one major subject of conversation, which continued to crop up in the days that followed, was the forthcoming crossing of the Puerto del Palo pass, at a height of more than 1200m. When you leave Campiello (the last *albergue* before the pass, since the one at Borres does not have a good reputation), there are two possible routes. Either you walk through Pola de Allande, in which case you can do the crossing in two days for there is an *albergue* at Pola; or, you take the direct route on the path of *Los Ospedales*, which means walking more than 25km without the least human dwelling in view. The name *Los Ospedales* refers in fact to the ruins of three medieval "hospitals". These were not hospitals in the medical sense, but places of hospitality built to shelter passing pilgrims. Despite the distance, the passage by *Los Ospedales* is physically easier, since there is only one long ascent of 9km, followed by the descent into Berducedo; if you go via Pola on the other hand, there is an ascent, followed by a descent into Pola, and then very a stiff climb before you get over the pass. The problem with the path by *Los Ospedales* is first that it can be difficult if there is rain or fog, and second that once you are committed to it, there is nowhere to stop on the way.

What to do? Everything drew me to *Los Ospedales* and I was not the only one: I love the wild open spaces of the mountains, where you are miles away from everything, and you can see far into the distance. But I also know that the mountains demand respect, that they can quickly become dangerous, and that clouds and mist can be treacherous. They come down and envelope you without warning. And then, what weather should we expect? Nobody could say. In the

Asturias, nobody knows what the weather will be like in two hours, let alone in two days… It was generally agreed that any decision could safely be put off until we reached Campiello.

Campiello is a funny place. There is nothing much but two *albergues*, each of which is also a bar, a restaurant, a little supermarket, and a warehouse selling agricultural supplies. They are situated at opposite ends of the village. One can only imagine the competition between them, and in my imagination Campiello became a sort of Asturian version of Clint Eastwood's *For a fistful of dollars*. A Spaniard who I walked with for a while recommended the Casa Herminiana, so that is where my backpack and I ended up for the night.

I hope you'll pardon me if I take a moment to talk about food. I haven't said much on the subject before, because the repetition of the *menú peregrino* (pilgrim's menu) that you find wherever you stop would soon become monotonous. The Casa Herminiana, however, is something else again. That evening we began with an *empanada* just to get the digestive juices working (it's a sort of bread roll with stuffing, often tuna); then, a soup; then another soup, good and thick with lentils; then an enormous paella dish filled with pasta, fish, and seafood (a good deal more pasta than seafood to be sure, but then the whole meal only cost €10); I thought that was the end, but not at all, in came another equally huge paella dish, this time full of chicken and potatoes; then dessert…

And the next morning, more of the same treatment: coffee, as many *tostadas* (thick slices of toast) as you could eat… I was surprised not to see any butter on the table, but the Señora (Herminiana herself, perhaps?) informed me that the toast was already soaked in olive oil. I confess that I had never before thought of combining jam with olive oil, but my word isn't it good!

Finally, I had to take my courage in both hands, leave behind me hot coffee and *tostadas*, and set out once again on the Way; this was the moment of truth, when the decision for or against the passage by

Los Ospedales would have to be taken. I got my pack on my back, stepped out the door… and all the conditions we had been warned against were there: it was foggy (or the clouds were very low, which comes to the same thing), the rain was not far off, and the weather forecast — for what that was worth here — was thoroughly discouraging.

I walked off. Looking around, I definitely had the feeling that I could see at least 20m, perhaps even 50m. And it wasn't actually raining, at least not yet. I was more and more convinced that the high road could be attempted, and when I came to the parting of the ways the choice was already made.

The path climbed upwards, as expected. I slowed my pace and lengthened my stride, everything was going fine. It began to rain; that too was expected. I got out all the gear: waterproof jacket and trousers, a waterproof cover for my pack. The higher I climbed the less I could see, I was rising into the clouds which completely hid the countryside I had just left behind me, and which must surely have been spread out below, somewhere. As fast as the wind chased the clouds away, so more clouds came galloping up like wild horses from the valleys, and over the crest of the hill.

I passed by the ruins of the first *Ospedal*, there was so little to see that I would have missed it completely had it not been for the signpost. A herd of cows watched me pass. Their bells, the wind, my steps on the stony path, the creaking straps on my backpack, were all I could hear. The other pilgrims were either in front of me, or behind, at all events they were completely out of sight. I was alone in the world.

A few slopes later, as if by magic, the wind stripped away the veil of clouds and I gazed far into the distance. Not a house in sight, no trace of human activity other than the Way reaching away at my feet, to the other side of the mountains. They stretched before me towards the horizon, wild and sublime.

Suddenly, I was filled with the oceanic feeling that Freud spoke of, a feeling of belonging in the natural world, whose millennia immeasurably surpass our individual existence, or even that of our species. All the negative emotions that we accumulate in the course of our existence seemed to fall away, washed away by the rain, carried off in the clouds which seemed to flee, chased into rags by the wind. Such emotions — anger, disgust, frustration, resentment even — are probably inevitable, even necessary; they are surely part of our mental defences against the world, just as our immune system produces antibodies to battle invasive organisms. But just like the immune system, our psychological defences can suffer from overload and even produce allergic reactions. It's not for nothing that we have the expression "gut reaction" for moments when we fly off the handle. These reactions reinforce our feelings of alienation from our fellows and from the natural world to which we belong, an alienation which has been part of the human condition ever since humanity existed.

I knew that this feeling of breaking through the walls of separation, of alienation, could only be fleeting. You can't live forever in transcendance, nonetheless I wanted to hang on to it, I tried to drink it in as much as I could. Perhaps, I would be able to take away some shreds, a tenuous memory, an inspiration from the state of mind that came to me in those cloud-covered, windswept heights.

Shortly afterwards, the rain came down again, this time in buckets. At the entrance to the first tiny hamlet after the pass, built all in glistening black stone and apparently deserted, four of our group from Bodenaya found shelter briefly in the porch of a chapel: with me were a Belgian, and two Germans who had somehow lost their way on the mountain. We were all soaked, the rain was beginning to penetrate our waterproofs, and the temperature had dropped considerably. But there was nothing to be done, we could only go on, down paths transformed into veritable rivulets where the water came up to our ankles. Never had an *albergue* been more welcome than the first bar in Berducedo which welcomed us warmly in with the luxuries of a hot-air drier to dry our boots, a hot shower to revive our bodies, and a solid meal to care for the inner man.

The next day dawned in bright sunshine, hot already in the early morning. A few clouds in the sky seemed to be there merely for dramatic effect. The Way rose up towards the summits of the mountains. The Asturias opened up to me in all their verdant splendour.

I had decided to offer myself an easy day's walk into Grandas da Salime. My guardian angel must have been my inspiration: not only did the ascents and descents on the path turn out to be much more taxing than I had expected, Grandas itself turned out to be a charming little town which is well worth a stop (expecially at the Casa Sanchez, an agreeable *albergue* with a garden to sit in). Grandas has an interesting ethnographic museum displaying aspects of Spanish rural life in the 1950s. I was thus able to climb into one of the *horreos* which had aroused my curiosity and which you see throughout the countryside; they're a sort of small barn perched on stone mushrooms which keep out the rodents and other pests. It was striking too, to see the reconstitution of a 1950s classroom, with of course the obligatory photo of Franco on the wall, and a few newspapers vaunting the Caudillo's prowess — a ponderous propaganda for simpletons, what democratic progress has been made since then!

By one of those happy chances which is part of the Camino's charm, that evening a youth choir was singing in the church, with a repertoire of songs both secular and religious. What joy it was to listen to those clear young voices, and even more to see what pleasure they took themselves in the song! And to think that if I had not been so tired as a result of the previous day, I would have pressed on to Castro and missed their performance!

I pass briefly over the days that followed, until my arrival in Lugo. The countryside was still magnificent, but I didn't find the towns of A Fonsagrada and O Cadavo particularly interesting. And it started raining again, or rather, it rained every afternoon. The previous year, it occurred to me, I set out at 06:30 in the morning to avoid the heat; this year, I started early to get under cover before the rain began at 15:00.

It's worth stopping at Lugo. The old town is still surrounded by its Roman walls, the walk along the top is a spectacular 2km tour. In a little museum next to the cathedral you can see the remains of a Roman villa. There is not a great deal to see, but a short film (which they ran in English especially for me, the only non Spanish speaker in the place) gives an interesting explanation of the ruins you see around you.

Then the town itself is agreeable too, full of people strolling about, relaxing in the bars and restaurants. I just missed the annual town fete where the entire population dress up as Romans and put on shows and processions, in honour of Lugo's glorious Roman past. I only witnessed the preparations, with practice processions of Roman legionaries, but it was the barbarian auxiliaries who seemed to be having the most fun.

The *horreos* puzzled me. In the Asturias they are generally square, about the size of a large room but with a low roof. In Galicia they are long and rectangular. Why such a difference? I have no idea. But shortly before arriving in Lugo the *horreos* all disappeared, in their place were remarkable round barns all built in slate, reminiscent of the round towers of Lugo's city wall.

After Lugo, I saw them no longer. Was it really a coincidence? Were the local farmers inspired by Lugo's ancient Roman walls, or was it the other way round?

Now, on the road out of Lugo, I must leave you. Shortly after, at Melide, the Primitivo joins the Camino Francés (or perhaps we should say that the Francés joins the Primitivo, which is the older of the two after all), and the pilgrim's Way becomes a highway. But Way's end, in Santiago, will be for later.

I receive the benediction

No believer me, yet on the Way I received the church's benediction.

It happened in Laredo, shortly after I had left Bilbao. The first *albergue* you come to on entering the town is right up against the church, and is run by the Sisters of the Trinity (I have no idea what distinguishes the Sisters of the Trinity from the plethora of other religious orders in the Catholic Church).

They were so amiable, the Sisters. Some of them were even young, which is rare; very different from the monastery where I stayed after Markina Xemein, where the four surviving monks were all thoroughly venerable. After the usual formalities, the Sisters informed me that a special mass would be held for the pilgrims, and gave me the impression that this was important for them. I felt almost obligated to attend if only out of politeness, I didn't want to hurt their feelings and the price of the bed was so absurdly low that I felt more like a guest than a customer.

I also confess to a certain ethnographic curiosity. Apart perhaps from Poland, Spain is surely Europe's most Catholic country, and yet the churches almost everywhere are kept locked. So the opportunity to see the inside of a church, and to witness the ceremony, and still more to do so not as a mere spectator but as a participant, a blessed pilgrim, seemed too good to miss.

Then there was this sensation, which often came to me on the Way, of treading in the steps of all the centuries that had gone before, that I was connected to all those pilgrims who had preceded me and who must have felt so powerfully the need of benediction and of God's protection on their Way. I hoped, somehow, to see the world through their eyes by taking part in their ceremony.

What sent them out on the Way? I often wondered. No doubt for many, it was religious fervour, or to do penance for some crime and thus earn the forgiveness of the Church, perhaps sometimes just from a taste for adventure and exotic countries. There were some who were paid to do the pilgrimage by the wealthy and impenitent. And there were those who lived on the Way by swindling and fleecing honest pilgrims.

So then, for all those reasons, I ended up attending a Catholic Mass for the first time in my life.

Now that Mass is no longer said in Latin, I could pretty much follow the ceremony in Spanish, and it was almost identical to my childhood memories of the Anglican Communion, with one exception: in the Communion everybody gets to drink the wine, in the Catholic Mass only the priest does. I realised that it all left me completely indifferent, that it seemed hollow, as empty as the church itself, a fine building capable of holding a congregation twenty times greater than the handful of faithful actually present. The feeling of emptiness was accentuated by the fact that everything was amplified by loudspeakers, which shouldn't be necessary in churches that are constructed expressly to resonate with the human voice. As if the social evolution which has emptied the churches of their congregations had also emptied their ceremonies of their significance.

It was only towards the end, when the congregation stood up to leave, and the five pilgrims present advanced towards the altar, that I felt touched, not by grace, but by humanity. Looking into the priest's eyes, I found his face gentle, serious, kindly, and so I received the benediction not so much of the Church but of another human being, who without knowing me, wished me well on my Way.

I come here to the conclusion of this little episode, and feel the need of a little pick-me-up by way of an antidote. What better than to listen to *"Tempête dans un bénitier"* composed by the very unsaintly Georges Brassens shortly after the Church allowed Mass to be celebrated in the vernacular (this scandalised the traditionalists at the time and does so even to this day), which seems to me wholly appropriate…

> *Sans le latin, sans le latin*
> *Plus de mystère magique*
> *Le rite qui nous envoûte*
> *S'avère alors anodin*
> *Sans le latin, sans le latin*
> *Et les fidèl's s'en foutent*
> *O très Sainte Marie mèr' de*
> *Dieu, dites à ces putains*
> *De moines qu'ils nous emmerdent*
> *Sans le latin*[9]

---

[9] Without Latin / no more magical mystique / the rite that once bewitched us / just seems boring and dull / and the faithful don't care any more / O Mary Mother of God / tell these bloody / monks that they get on our nerves / without Latin

Altamira, our origins, tourism

At Santillana del Mar I stopped for two nights, to give myself a whole day for a visit to the painted caves of Altamira.

You might wonder what is the point of studying cave paintings made more than 15,000 years ago, at a time when the whole planet (or at least, our ability to live on it) is threatened by global warming and the ecological insanity of unbridled capitalism. Of course, there's the sheer pleasure of it, which needs no justification. But there's more too: for me, we need to try to understand our ancestors' past, and the messages that they unintentionally left us, because what science reveals of their lives can be a useful remedy for the commonplace prejudices you hear everywhere these days, about "human nature".

The paintings were discovered in 1879 by Marcelino Sanz de Sautuola, or rather by his eight year old daughter. The story is not without irony. Sanz de Sautuola had already been exploring the caves for some years without finding anything very significant, and it was only when he brought his little girl with him, that the child's gaze turned upwards to the ceiling, where she saw an extraordinary collection of paintings.

When Sanz de Sautuloa first published his findings a year later, the scientific community of the day refused to believe him; he was even accused of fabrication. The undeniable artistic quality of the caves did not fit at all with contemporary theories about the barbaric and under-developed nature of "primitive" man. In my view, this was no accident: Sanz de Sautuloa made his discovery in the last quarter of the 19th century, in the midst of the "race for Africa" by European, notably British and French, imperialism. The ideological justification for this orgy of conquest, rapine, and generalised vandalism was the "civilising mission" of Europeans on behalf of "savage" and "primitive" peoples. This justification was hard to maintain in the face of the sophistication of the paintings executed by a human culture which was a good deal more primitive than the cultures of Mali, Morocco, Benin, etc, then being subjected to conquest and "civilisation". Only when the paintings of Altamira were followed by other discoveries, did their authenticity become undeniable. And as equally remarkable discoveries (such as Lascaux) were made in France, French prestige could lay claim to new and illustrious ancestors.

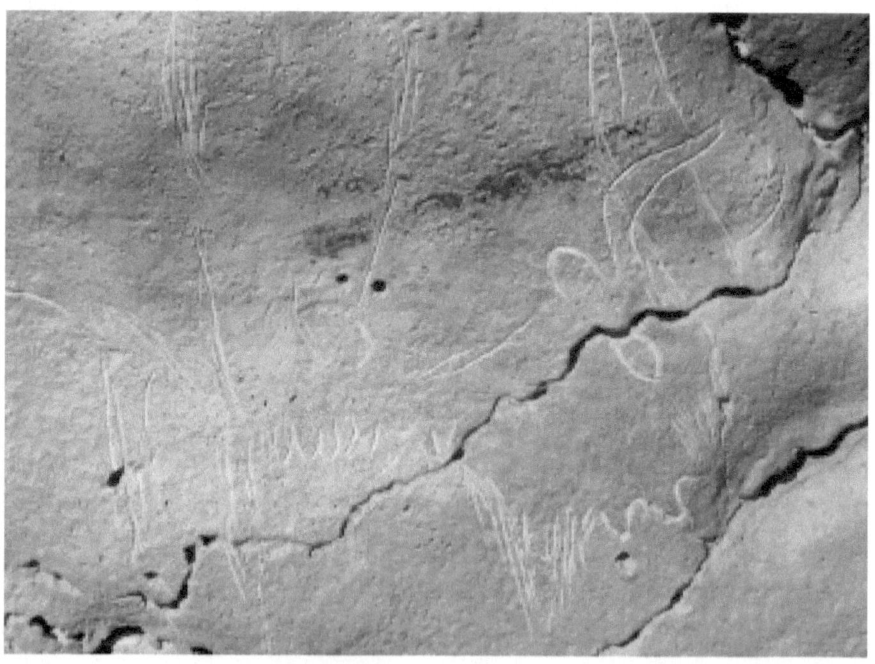

I had seen the Lascaux caves as a child, but I was too young to remember much, and my memories have probably been too mixed up with those of a photo from Lascaux which hung for many years on the wall of my parents' sitting-room. I had seen reproductions of course, but nothing had prepared me for seeing them "for real", *in situ*. It is not for nothing that Altamira was called "The Sixtine Chapel of the Palaeolithic". On the artistic level, this is absolutely not a condescending compliment paid by the "civilised" to the "primitive", as one might congratulate a child. These images are worthy of the greatest works of the human imagination.

What struck me most forcibly was their extraordinary confidence of line. Often, the artist would begin a painting by drawing an outline sketch, engraving it directly onto the rock. Look at the sketch on the previous page; there is not an erasure to be seen, not a single mistake. Every line is powerful and true. And now, look at this sketch by Picasso:

One of the 20th century's greatest painters possessed the same gestural power as those unknown artists of 15,000 years ago.

How did they (men or women, since in Altamira there is no indication of the artists' sex) achieve such a level of artistic sophistication? This question has been haunting me ever since. Picasso was the heir to a whole European artistic tradition on which he could draw, and of which he was both the outcome and the critical and revolutionary overthrow. From whom, from what tradition, did the masters of Altamira inherit?

What was their status within palaeolithic society? There is one immediately obvious difference between the two images: Picasso's is signed, so straight away we are in a world where the artist himself is an image within the social imagination, of a solitary individual genius, but also where his work is an object of value, of speculation and hoarding. The artist's status, but also that of his work, is thus very different in archaic society and in our own. That aside, it is obvious that these paintings are not the mere scribblings of "primitives", on the contrary these artists must have undergone a severe process of apprenticeship and selection. Not every modern artist has Picasso's genius, and there is no reason to suppose that human beings were any different 15,000 years ago. Moreover, there are other caves in the region where the paintings are clearly of the same inspiration but lesser quality, rather as we might compare the decoration of a minor parish church to that of St Peter's in Rome. Altamira must then have been an exceptional place which attracted the greatest artists. How did that happen?

Surely they were not just artists. It is only in the modern world that art has become something separated from everyday life, that it no longer has a directly social function as did, for example, the frescoes in medieval churches. Art today still has a function, of course, but it is less direct, artistic execution is further removed, so to speak, from day to day life. The masters of Altamira must have fulfilled a ritual function within their society, but what? Personally, I lean rather to the theory proposed by Jean Clottes and David Lewis-Williams, which sees these paintings as expressions of shamanism. Contrary to what was at first imagined, the paintings do not illustrate the hunters' prey (the remains discovered at the sites have shown that the most painted animals were rarely hunted), but rather the shaman's familiar spirits in animal form.

Were the artists men or women? Impossible to tell of course, although we glean some clues from the Chauvet caves in France. In Chauvet, there are a large number of negative hand images, created by placing the hand against the rock face and blowing powdered ochre onto the surface. Since in general, male hands have a greater difference in length between the index and the ring fingers than female hands, researchers have concluded that at least one of the artists must have been a woman. And this fits the reality observed in many societies with shamanistic beliefs, and where the function of the shaman may be performed indifferently by men or women.

How are we to explain that this degree of artistic skill seems not to have been attained anywhere other than Europe (with the possible exception of Australia, about which I know too little to have an opinion)? The oldest figurative art in the world dates back more than 40,000 years and is to be found in Lubank Jeriji Saléh in the Indonesian province of East Kalimatan. There are thousands of decorated sites, all over the world. Yet nowhere else but Europe, to my knowledge, have they reached such a degree of sophistication. Is it just a lucky chance, that in Europe the artists decorated caves where they were preserved undisturbed for millennia? Or maybe the European societies' beliefs attributed special value to such images, and so encouraged a constant search for greater perfection?

Another question: what is the significance of the undeniable similarity of artistic style that unites the caves of Altamira, Chauvet, Lascaux and others? This unity is indeed remarkable when we consider that it covers a vast geographic area, and a length of time to make you dizzy. The oldest Chauvet paintings date from 37,000 years ago. What are we to make of a cultural unity that lasted for more than 15,000 years? If you think that in a mere 10,000 years, we have progressed from the beginnings of agriculture to the technical application of quantum mechanics, such a degree of social stability is barely imaginable. How was it possible? What are the implications for our own ability to manage psychologically the constant social upheaval to which we ourselves are subjected? Could art help us, and if so, how?

On reproductions and mass tourism

And now, I have a confession to make: I never saw the caves of Altamira. I went there, and I visited the museum, but the paintings can only be seen in reproduction. As at Lascaux, it was found that the repeated passage of visitors brought with it humidity and bacteria which endangered the paintings; they had only survived so long thanks to the collapse of the cave entrance which kept them walled off for millennia. It was therefore decided to create a copy, as faithful as possible, of the entire cave, reproducing not just the paintings but the whole rock surface right down to its tiniest crack. The same has been done at Chauvet, which was closed with an airlock to all but a small team of archaeologists, as soon as it was discovered.

The reproduction is remarkably well done, I'm even inclined to think that it is better than the original, inasmuch as the cave has been restored as it was before it collapsed, with a diorama of a human habitat in the entrance. Apparently, and unlike Chauvet where the people lived some distance from the caves which they had to share with bears, Altamira was inhabited for a significant part of its history. Who were these people? Were they the artists? Doubtless we will never know.

But this business of reproduction takes me back to a discussion with my English artist friend Jeff, when last he came through Paris. He had put me on to the writings of the art critic John Berger, which impressed me hugely. I was struck especially by Berger's proposal to make more use of reproductions in museums, the better to make great works of art accessible to all. Why not, after all? Why not make multiple copies of the Mona Lisa and distribute them to museums all around the world? Indeed, with the technologies available today, the copies could be more than perfect: it would surely be possible, with a sufficiently painstaking analysis of the original's chemical composition, to show us Mona Lisa not as we see her today, dulled by the accumulated patina of centuries, but bright and fresh as she emerged from Leonardo's studio. Rather as here at Altamira, I have been offered a view of the caves as they might have appeared to our ancestors.

Jeff didn't agree; for him, there is always something special about the original. You can distinguish the trace of the brush, in a certain sense you can communicate directly with the artist, rather, perhaps, as I sometimes seem to feel under my feet the trace of all those pilgrims who preceded me over the centuries. Nor can I really say that Jeff is entirely wrong, I perfectly understand his desire to communicate with the past, with the other, even more so when you are obliged to make the journey especially. That said, Berger is also undoubtedly right when he says that one of the main reasons for enforcing copyright and tracking down fakes is simply because the artistic value of the original has been submerged by its cash value as a portable object of investment and speculation.

Of course Altamira, like Lascaux and Chauvet, is a special case. Here there was no choice: without the copy the original would have been destroyed, and nobody would have seen it at all.

But isn't this also what has happened to the Mona Lisa, in a certain sense? The scene, if you try to see the painting in the Louvre today, is grotesque. The room is invaded by a huge crowd, and everyone is trying desperately to make their way to the front to take their place, for an instant, in front of the iconic picture. Unable to see the picture, they raise their telephones on selfie-sticks in the hopes of taking home in triumph not just the proof that they have seen the Mona Lisa, but that they were there, themselves, in front of it. In such conditions, any individual relationship with the painting or the artist is impossible, there is no room for contemplation. Would it not then be better to make reproductions to be hung in the world's great museums to allow more people to see it, in the proper conditions which are no longer possible today? This is what they have done with Altamira in fact, since there is said to be an exact copy of the cave's reproduction in Munich.

I'm getting off my subject, so perhaps this is where I should stop. Or perhaps not; perhaps this is rather where I should return to the question of mass tourism.

I came up against this regularly along the Way. To start with, the subject was in the news that year, on the rare occasions when I came back online: demonstrations in Barcelona against AirBnB, restrictions on holiday rentals imposed by the city of Berlin, people complaining that they no longer feel at home in their own town because housing in the tourist areas has become too expensive. Then more immediately, there was that discussion the year before in the hostel at Périgueux concerning the "touristification" of the Camino, my own feelings of unease at the site of all those packs that pilgrims were unable or unwilling to carry by themselves, dumped in the *albergues* by the specialised transport companies, the transformation of Bilbao, the experience of the pilgrim highway into Compostela.

Reading Jean-Christophe Rufin's book left me feeling ambivalent.

To be honest, I didn't like his book very much. Or rather, there were aspects of Rufin's personality that I didn't like very much. I got the impression that he was too pleased with himself for walking "the hard way", that is to say sleeping outside in a tent or under the stars; I didn't like the way he looked down, from the great height of his own good opinion of himself, on all the other pilgrims who were not walking far enough to deserve his good graces, and I especially disliked his disdain for the tourists that made him flee Santillana del Mar: the disdain typical of those who have had the good fortune to acquire high culture, for those who have not.

When it comes to traveling, I've been very fortunate. What with the travels with my father as a child, those I undertook myself, and those where I was sent for work, I have set foot on every continent on the planet, with the exception of the Antarctic and sub-Saharan Africa. My father liked to say of his family that "We are travellers, not tourists", and as a child of course I adopted the same viewpoint; nor was it wholly unjustified, since my father took his family with him on journeys to countries where travelling was not necessarily easy or even safe. Yet nonetheless, I've never been able to get rid of a certain discomfort when I think of his words: it's so easy after all, and so agreeable, to adopt this attitude of superiority towards the sheeplike crowds of tourists... But in truth, from time to time, tourists we were.

As an adult, and without really thinking about it, I was simply unconditionally in favour of everybody travelling as much as possible, whatever the circumstances. "Travelling educates youth" says the French proverb, and not just youth. I felt that travelling could only do people good by broadening their horizons and improving their knowledge of whatever is different from home. I remember a friend's parents, who had never been able to travel when young (they were of the 1930s generation and Spanish to boot) and who, on their retirement, went off regularly on package coach tours, exactly the kind of tourism that my father would have detested. But isn't it a bit much to ask of people who have no experience of foreign countries, who speak no foreign languages, who barely know their own country outside their own region, to become adventurers in their old age? On the contrary, bravo I thought for package tours which made it possible for them to see something different.

Having grown up in Oxford, I'm well placed to judge of the changes wrought by mass tourism. If I take a mental stroll through the home town of my youth, how different it has become today! Back then, Oxford was not really a tourist destination. The motorway linking it to London didn't exist, the trains still used steam locomotives and not very comfortable coaches. The town itself was blackened by smoke from the coal fires which heated the houses, and ran the trains and the factory, you could barely make out the original colour of the ancient colleges' stonework under its patina of soot.

Broad Street was full of bookshops: a whole section of the street was occupied by Blackwells the publisher, leaning against the University Library. Opposite, there was a bookshop devoted to the visual arts, and another selling nothing but paperbacks. And all these bookshops occupied several floors. The ultimate bookshop for me, was Thornton's. There were new books on the ground floor, but the three upper stories were crammed from floor to ceiling with second-hand books. Even the narrow staircase was made narrower still by shelves that stretched, packed tight with books, right up to the ceiling.

As a young adolescent, I took it into my head to learn Farsi (the language spoken in Iran); by the age of 17 I had reached the point where I wanted to attempt the great Persian poet Sa'adi, in the original. So I went to Thornton's (where else?), and explained what I was looking for. The bookseller thought for a moment, then said very calmly, as if my request were the most normal thing in the world, "Well, if you go to the first floor, take the first door on your right, then you should find what you want on the shelf immediately above the fireplace, roughly in the middle". I followed his instructions and found my book. "That", I said to myself, "is a real bookshop". Nor was Thornton's the only second-hand bookshop, the covered market had two or three more of them.

Next to Thornton's stood my childhood Nirvana: Howes' model shop, full of model trains and planes.

I loved to go shopping with my mother in the covered market. The coffee shop still roasted its own coffee, and the warm smell wafted out from the market into the surrounding streets; inside, you could find an unimaginable variety of teas from every corner of the world. The townsfolk did their shopping in the market: at the butchers, the fishmongers, the grocers, the flower shops, even the delicatessen which sold exotic foods imported from "the Continent" (in other words, from France, Germany, or Italy). There were two little cafés that sold the "full English breakfast", all day.

Oxford had the usual tobacconists of course, but there were also two shops in the High Street, almost next door to each other, that specialised in exotic tobacco. You could buy French cigarettes, naturally, but also cigarettes from Russia, Turkey, or Egypt; these last came in tin boxes of 400, and could be bought singly.

An English university town without pubs is inconceivable, and I frequented them as soon as I was old enough to be an underage drinker. There was the Turf Tavern, hidden down a tiny alleyway and inaccessible from the street, an ancient pub huddled under the medieval city walls; the Bear, which dated back to the 13th century and was barely big enough to hold a dozen students; the White Horse, stuck between two bookshops, with its low ceiling and wooden beams blackened by smoke; the Eagle and Child, with its two snugs at the entrance, each of them barely capable of seating half a dozen people, and where CS Lewis and Tolkien sketched out their novels; and then, further out from the centre, there were the White House, the Marlborough Arms, the White Hart, the Gardener's Arms, the Trout and the Perch… and those were just my own favourite haunts. They were all devoted to the consumption of beer, of course (pubs were not eating places in those days), but above all to conviviality and the conversation of friends. I've lost count of the number of times that we remade the world over a pint, or two, or three.

During the week, most of the traffic in the city streets was made up of students and teachers making their way to their classes on foot or by bike. But Oxford was not just a university town, it was also an industrial one with one of the country's biggest car factories, and on the weekends the centre filled up with workers and their families from the industrial suburbs, come in to shop or just to have fun, a crowd of people in holiday mood but not overbearing.

So what is Oxford like today?

The coal fires are gone, the colleges have been cleaned and restored and appear once again to us in all their beauty, for the greater pleasure of the tourists who come in their millions — 7 million every year to be precise — on the motorway that now links Oxford with London and Birmingham, or by the train which brings you from London in one hour. Inevitably, 7 million visitors every year changes the face of a town of only 150,000 inhabitants, even more so when they are all crammed into a city centre that dates from the Middle Ages and was never intended to fit so many people. Now you can eat in all the pubs, which have doubled or tripled in size and lost a good deal of their intimacy, or else been converted into trendy hotels whose atmosphere does not encourage remaking the world; the paperback shop now only sells postcards and tat for tourists, as does the model shop, one of the specialist tobacconists, and a good part of the covered market. Thornton's (*o tempora, o mores!*) has been converted into a sandwich bar. The colleges where once you entered freely now charge a fee and are often closed to visitors (apparently it disturbs the students, who sometimes study in their spare time). Housing in Oxford is some of the most expensive in the country. In short, the town is greatly changed. And even if I wish the tourists well, and even if I'm delighted at the pleasure they find strolling through my home town, I can't help missing the town that is no longer. The fact is that Oxford, like any ancient city, simply was not built to welcome millions of visitors every year; its old city centre must have seen at most a few thousands pass through, coming to the annual fair of St Giles, or to the weekly cattle market (which reminds me, back in the day, down by the cattle market there were a couple of pubs with a special dispensation allowing them to stay open all day, on market days — another little local curiosity, disappeared long ago).

I've gone into some detail because Oxford is a town which I have seen change over the years. I wonder if the inhabitants of Bilbao feel the same? Oxford, it's true, has not suffered the same industrial and urban collapse (or at least not on the same scale: the Morris car factory, which employed 20,000 workers in the 1970s, now belongs to BMW and employs less than 5000). Do the inhabitants of the Casco Viejo regret the influx of tourists, and of pilgrims like me? Are they condemned to the same fate as the inhabitants of Barcelona and the Barrio Chino? It seems that the Casco Viejo has already become an expensive district.

Then what about all the country towns trying to do the same thing as Bilbao on a smaller scale, in other words to pretty themselves up, or to attract visitors with cultural events? Sometimes it works. Since 1988, the little town of Hay-on-Wye, on the frontier between England and Wales, has held an annual literary festival, and has become known world wide for its bookshops; indeed, it must be the only town in the country with more bookshops than pubs.

So far I've only mentioned what you might call "cultural tourism". People go to see towns that are well-known, or have managed to make themselves known. In China it seems, the fashion is to visit sites adopted by UNESCO, and not just in China either; you hear people talking about their "bucket lists" of places to see, just to be able to tick another one off the list. Then of course there's another kind of tourism, "tanning tourism" you might call it. Since the 1960s, the whole south coast of Spain has been concreted over to build roads, houses, apartment blocks right on the seafront, in order to accommodate the armies of tourists who come for the sun, to eat and drink cheap, and nothing else. Now that the beaches are full, mass tourism has taken to the high seas in enormous cruise ships that sail around the world, leaving trails of garbage and pollution in their wake. Not even the summit of Everest is immune.

In St Jean Pied de Port, somebody had stuck a notice on their front door on which I read these words:

> *Tourism is a sub-product of the circulation of commodities, the circulation of human beings as a consumer product; fundamentally it has been reduced to the leisure to go and see what has already become banal. The planning inherent in the tourist economy is in itself a guarantee that the places visited all become the same. The same modernisation that has eliminated from the journey the reality of time, has also eliminated the reality of space.*

I have no idea who wrote these lines and pinned them up, but they are right on target. Mass travel is cut-price industrialised travel, always. Tourists travel closed up in the shell of their plane, their coach, their hotel identical to thousands of other hotels around the world. When you arrive at your destination, you already know what you're going to see and even what you're going to think of it because you've already seen the photos and read the comments on Tripadvisor. You're greeted everywhere by the same shop signs, the same products, you can buy the same T-shirts with just a difference in slogan to show where they come from. You can eat the same more or less familiar food, whose tastes have been toned down to avoid shocking the tourist palate and because the ingredients are all industrialised, and so on, and on.

But as the unknown protestor of St Jean Pied de Port says, mass tourism is merely another expression of the generalised massification of society as a whole.

My father used to do a lot of handiwork about the house, and when I was little I sometimes used to accompany him to the iron-monger's. It seemed huge to my child's eyes, and indeed I think it really was quite big. More than anything, I remember the smell, a rich mixture of floor wax, sawdust, and all kinds of products like creosote, or that revolting sulphur that my father used to spray on the gooseberry bushes to discourage the insects and the birds. The shop disappeared long ago, and of course it has been replaced by a banal shopping centre full of the same shops, the same products, the same mass consumption as everywhere else.

More than anything, mass consumption sells the biggest illusion of our day: the illusion of freedom. The vast majority of working people are of course salaried employees, and the principle of salaried work is that you sell to your employer, for the duration of the working day, your free will and your ability to choose what to do. Why do people flock in such masses to the shopping malls? Because there, you are not at work, you can stroll about and spend your money as you see fit; there, you are free. Better still you are both free and protected: protected from bad weather because the malls are always overheated, protected from disappointment because the products are always the same, and indeed you already know what you're getting because you've seen the advertisements or the disguised publicity of the "influencers" as they're called. And we want to be protected, especially against disappointment: life is too short and our free time is measured out too meanly for us to take the risk of being disappointed during this little space of liberty that we've been allowed. It's the same when you travel. For a week or two, you have the right to escape the stress of wage labour, to store up memories which will belong to you. Perhaps that is the wellspring of "selfie mania": you must have a picture of yourself standing in front of a monument, to convince yourself that you were really there; photograph yourself having fun, otherwise you would not be certain whether you were having fun or not. Live the dream that Andy Warhol imagined, where anybody can be famous for five minutes. Or perhaps we do this because, more than ever, it is forbidden to be unhappy, and because we must, at all costs, elevate ourselves to the implacable level of happiness of the TV commercials and the influencers.

Am I going to look down on people who travel like that? Absolutely not! I too go shopping in the malls, I too have been a tourist in foreign cities and stayed in AirBnBs, I too have been on package holidays.

We will only escape from social massification in a society where the mass can become individuals. But until that day comes, we can at least think more about our reasons for travelling. And take risks.

Nicolas Bouvier said it very well in his account of Japan, *Le vide et le plein*:

> *Too many people expect everything of their journey, without ever thinking about what the journey expects of them. They hope that a change of scene will cure them of inadequacies which are not national, but human, and the intoxication of the first weeks where since everything is new, you have the impression that you yourself are renewed, give them the passing feeling that their hopes have been granted. But when the ego, which they had hoped to leave discreetly behind them at the railway station or the harbour, catches them up in some foreign landscape, then they blame this country where they have chosen to live for the return of that morose and solitary ego which they thought to have sloughed off.*
> *The journey will teach you nothing if you don't also give it the chance to demolish you. It's a rule that's as old as the world. A journey is like a shipwreck, and those who have never been wrecked know nothing of the sea. Anything else is just sliding over the surface, or tourism.*

Language and cultural diversity

When I was younger, and even until quite recently, I imagined a world united by a single language. Talking to my friend Amaïa in Bilbao changed my mind and made me realise that I had seen things too simply, not to say simplistically.

Taking as my starting point the principle that language is intended for human beings to communicate with each other, and my ardent hope to see humanity one distant day united without any distinction between nations, it seemed to me logical to suppose that all the minority or regional languages (such as Basque, Breton, Welsh, French or Italian…) would disappear little by little to meld into one common world language. This language would of course be the only currently existing international language, that is to say English, even if this would be an English enriched beyond recognition by contributions from all the other, by now outdated, languages on the planet. English seemed to me all the better adapted to play such a role, in that it adopts with disconcerting ease, expressions and words from elsewhere, and is not encumbered by a lot of the grammatical rules that I find so tedious in French. The serenity with which I envisaged the disappearance of so much of humanity's linguistic heritage is perhaps not unrelated to the fact that English is my mother tongue…

As the years went by, my certainty on this score began to fade. First of all, I realised how easily children in the right environment are able to learn several languages at once. Then one day, I asked an anthropologist among my acquaintances how he would explain the fact that we have retained this ability which sometimes seems so extraordinary, and which must have a cost for our brain, which already uses up an enormous 20% of our calorific intake. Quite simply, was his reply: the exogamic principle which is universal among archaic peoples would certainly mean that children would all have parents speaking different languages, so that growing up bilingual (at least) would have been normal to the point of banality.

Along the Way, I often had the feeling of being linguistically privileged: English is my mother tongue, French my adopted language, and my Spanish is good enough to get by, or even to keep up a limited conversation. So I am reasonably at ease in the Camino's *lingua franca*, and in the languages of the two countries I walked through. All this made me wonder one day, what it was like in the Middle Ages: Europe, after all, was much richer linguistically in those days. In France alone (or rather, in the region that today is called France) people not only spoke Breton, Basque, Flemish and Alsatian, but a plethora of dialects of the Langues d'Oc and d'Oïl (that is to say, Occitan and the ancestor of modern French), oh yes, and Provençal of course. In Germany, it is only in recent years that all the various dialects have begun to retreat before the standard Hochdeutsch. In the Iberian peninsula alone, the pilgrims would have crossed regions speaking multiple languages: Castilian, Basque, Asturian, Galego…

It can't just have been a problem for the pilgrims. How did the bankers and merchants communicate during the great fairs of Champagne (or of Provins, just near Paris)? They came from all over Europe, and these fairs were much bigger than the Christmas markets that our municipalities like to organise these days in France; they were veritable clearing houses, were the credits and debits accumulated during a year's commercial dealing were settled and paid. The merchants who went on business from town to town had to adapt to local laws, even to local weights and measures, and certainly to local languages and dialects as well. Then there were the journeymen who criss-crossed Europe to build its cathedrals; how did they manage to communicate?

Were they just better at languages than us? Then again, I walked for several days in the company of a German factory worker who had only studied four years of English at school, and yet spoke the language remarkably well.

Of course, there was one common language: Latin. But this was reserved for the educated elite, the clerks. How did everybody else get along? I can't help thinking that it must have been not uncommon to speak multiple languages.

In the 12th century kingdom of Sicily, the government's official documents were drawn up in Latin, Greek, and Arabic.

In the Ottoman Empire, people did not speak Turkic languages alone, far from it. They also spoke Armenian, Greek, Kurdish, Arabic, Syriac and Laze, amongst many others. The Empire's first socialist newspaper was published in Ladino, a Sephardic language.

Languages evolve. After the Norman conquest, among the "English" (who did not yet think of themselves as English), the common people spoke Saxon dialects related to Frisian while the nobles spoke a Norman dialect of old French. It wasn't until the end of the 14th century that Chaucer's famous Canterbury Tales appeared, and this is the first work written in an English which is recognisable as such and comprehensible today; the Tales are important not just for their intrinsic quality, but because they mark the country's cultural unification, the end of the complete linguistic separation between the aristocracy and the rest of the population.

This unification was the fruit of a long and slow evolution, but by the 18th and 19th centuries, cultural and therefore linguistic unity became active policy for the newly emerging nation-states. The reason was in part military: wars were no longer fought by hordes of aristocratic cavalry backed up by mercenaries on foot, now they were confrontations between great masses of conscripted infantry. The essence of military science was to manoeuvre masses of men in line, in squares, able to advance or retreat, to turn right or left, all in good order. The soldiers thus had to understand the orders they were given. The need was industrial also. The great industrial towns and regions attracted peasants from all over, on their way to becoming workers, capitalism demanded manpower that was undifferentiated and interchangeable, capable — like soldiers — of understanding orders.

The need for linguistic unity was also political. The "multicultural" empires, to use a modern expression (the Holy Roman Empire, the Ottoman or the Chinese Empires, or Tsarist Russia, to mention just a few), were united not nationally, but culturally and dynastically. This was also true in France, which far from being "eternal" as some people like to say, was a jumble of dynastic acquisitions without any particular unity other than the person of the King. After the French Revolution, the new ruling class had to impose a new political unity, and this is how the nation was, so to speak, invented on the basis of a mythical history going back to "our ancestors the Gauls". The imposition by force of a single language was part of the process.

France is one of the countries that took the process furthest, with its secular, republican, and obligatory system of education. Any language other than French was banned in school, and an Académie Française created which dictated the correct and erroneous use of grammar, and even words. On two separate occasions along the Way, I met a Basque and a Breton of my own generation, who recounted the shock of arriving at school for the first time to find that the language they spoke at home in their peasant families, and the only language they knew, was forbidden. Another Breton lady remarked to me that from the linguistic standpoint, republican France was not so different from the Franco dictatorship in Spain. It's worth pointing out, moreover, how difficult it still is to find classes in Arabic in

French schools, despite the fact that it is now France's second spoken language.

Today, local languages are flourishing in Spain: Catalan, Basque, Galego, Valencians, to name a few. Ironically though, the same problems are still posed. For example, is Valencians a real language or just a regional variant of Catalan? And what about the Basque Country? Today, it is possible in Spain, and even in France, to pursue a secondary education in Basque, right up to doctorate level. And why not? There's just one little problem: the Basque Country, on both sides of the Pyrenees, is divided up into seven provinces, each with its own linguistic peculiarities.

This is why we find, in Bilbao's handsome Plaza Nueva, the Euskaltzaindia, in other words, the Academy of the Basque Language, whose function is the same as that of the Académie Française: to lay down the norms, and to ensure the linguistic uniformity of the seven provinces.

It is disconcertingly easy for the attachment to a language to mutate into a xenophobic attitude of exclusion. That too, I saw on the Way, one evening during a discussion between French speakers, among whom there was a *Québecois* bus driver from Montreal. He complained bitterly about the invasion of "his" town by immigrants speaking nothing but English, and took offense at being served in English, in the shops or bars of "his" Quebec. I know too, that in Belgium there are Flemish towns where the employees of the town hall are forbidden to talk to their francophone fellow citizens in French, despite the fact that they speak the language perfectly. In part, this is merely a petty revenge on history, since in its industrial heyday Belgium was dominated by the Walloon (ie, French speaking) provinces.

Would it really matter if all these "minority" languages disappeared? If we were to find ourselves in that future world of my youthful imagination where everybody spoke a sort of enriched English and could understand each other from one end of the planet to the other?

Amaïa pointed out to me, and I couldn't fault her, that every language is more than just a means of communication, it is an entire culture. To lose a language also means to lose a prism, a perspective, a way of looking at the world. My visit to Bilbao's Museum of Fine Arts the previous year, when the works of Basque artists so enthused me, had brought home to me the value of cultural diversity. Not that the Basque painters were better than the others, it is simply that they offer us a different, original, view of the world in which we live together, including when they express themselves using an international idiom.

Linguists often draw an analogy between linguistic and biological evolution. Some of the mechanisms seem to be similar in both cases. For example, in biology one of the principal drivers of speciation is geographical separation, which causes members of the same species to evolve differently in the different environments created by the new divide, towards new species. Similarly, we can see a "speciation" of languages when they are cut off from their original culture. Hence we get Québecois, which is sometimes incomprehensible for the French, or the Acadian French of New Brunswick which is completely so, and which itself has its own dialects: the brayon and the chiac.

Today, it is known that the loss of bio-diversity poses a threat to agriculture and to the resilience of life in general: genetic diversity makes possible a faster and more effective adaptation to new diseases, and its disappearance makes the biome, and so the plants on which we depend, more vulnerable to the evolution of bacteria and parasites.

Should we not also say that the disappearance or weakening of languages threatens our cultural bio-diversity? And that the loss of their different perspectives diminishes our natural defences against the tidal wave of homogenisation created by globalised capitalism?

I encountered an unexpected illustration, a confirmation even, of this intuition (I don't dare call it an idea, it is neither clear nor organised enough) one day when I had the good fortune to walk with a young Australian woman whose trade was art restoration, and who specialised in contemporary and aboriginal art (which is a pretty considerable diversity wrapped up in just one person!). We spoke of the proliferation of aboriginal languages in Australia, and the profound knowledge of the natural world that finds expression through them. I was already aware, for example, of the songs that have survived on the coast of the Northern Territories and which trace with remarkable precision the geography of regions submerged 7000 years ago by the rise in sea levels at the end of the last Ice Age. But my walking companion gave me two other striking examples. The first, was the successful use of preventive burning to prevent brush fires, based on techniques used for millennia by the aborigines. The second, was recent climate studies carried out by the national Bureau of Meteorology. Realising the limitations of the European seasonal schema (summer, autumn, winter, spring) applied to the Australian climate, the Bureau turned to local aboriginal languages for help, and found that these defined, much more appropriately, six different seasons.

When it comes down to it, the threat to our bio-diversity, whether natural or cultural, all derives from the same source. Agriculture, which was for millennia the essential relationship between humanity and the rest of nature, has become just another industry like all the others. As in any industry, the key words are: investment, profitability, productivity, output. The result is the immense prairies of Picardy or the Brie, where the soil, loaded with chemical fertilisers and pesticides and compacted by the passage of agricultural machinery, is losing its ecosystem and its resilience. Similarly at school, the curriculum gives pride of place to subjects considered useful to national competitiveness (technical, mathematical, scientific, and then English, except of course in England where there is less and less interest in foreign languages), at the expense of the arts, music, sport, everything in short which contributes to a child's growth into a fully rounded human being. Yet again: investment, profitability, productivity, output.

As I reread these lines, I confess, I find myself stuck in an insoluble contradiction. If one accepts the proposition — and for myself, it seems increasingly incontrovertible — that humanity's different languages are not only a source of wealth to the same degree as biological diversity, but also a means of resistance to cultural homogeneity, then that means they should be encouraged and cultivated. That in turn means increasing the cost of the education system (a bilingual education is inevitably more expensive), which goes directly against the demands of productivity, which is always the final criterion in a capitalist economy. Then again, to defend a language always carries with it the danger of sclerosis. In a world where exchange is more and more a planetary phenomenon, a living language can only mutate, adapt to new situations, integrate words, phrases, or concepts taken from others. You can see this with the incorporation of English directly into other languages; how long before we start to do the same with Chinese? In France, the "defence" of the French language plumbed the depths of the absurd with the Toubon Law of 1994 which made it obligatory, for example, for any advertisement that used fashionable English words to reference these words with a little star to indicate the French translation somewhere at the bottom of the poster, generally printed illegibly small.

In the end, I have no solution to offer, nor even a very clear idea of what is the problem I would like to resolve.

All I know is that human variety is a fine thing: "variety is the spice of life", as the expression has it. There's nothing for it but to give myself up to the pleasure of walking through this beautiful Basque countryside, or strolling in the streets of splendid Bilbao, of hearing around me, from time to time, people talking in a language which for me is perfectly incomprehensible, and to follow the signs marked "Done Jakue Bidea", knowing that these will guide me further down the Camino de Santiago, or the Chemin de St Jacques, or as we have it in English: St James' Way.

Way's end

For three years, I have walked towards Compostela without really believing I would ever arrive. Yet finally, here I am…

After Lugo, the Camino Primitivo sheds its mountain wildness. The Way descends gently towards the sea, the countryside is much less hilly and the land more intensively cultivated, you walk through large farms and small towns. For the last three years, every time I was asked how far I intended to go, I would answer that I was heading for Compostela, for on the Way you never know what might happen nor how far you will be able to go. But at last I reached the point where I almost began to believe in it; and I wondered, what would I find at the end of the Way?

I had been warned that the Way would change at Melide, the town where the much busier Camino Francés joins the Primitivo. Not only that, Melide comes shortly after Sarria which is just 100km from Compostela, and that is the minimum distance that gives the pilgrim on foot the right to claim his *Compostela*, the certificate that attests his completion of the pilgrimage. Through Melide then, pass also all those who set out from Sarria, to get their *Compostela* after a minimum of walking. So, I had been warned, but I still was taken aback by the crowds. The Way felt more like a motorway, with a constant flow of walkers and cyclists; I was rarely alone with nobody visible either in front or behind. The path itself is agreeable enough, made of broad trails of beaten earth, often through woodland, with tarmac relatively rare. But the days of solitude and contemplation were over, and the paths of mud and scree that had taken me through the Asturias, with difficulty sometimes it's true, seemed far behind.

As for the pilgrims, many of them looked to me altogether too clean, with their little bags for a day out walking. The entrance to the evening's *albergue* too often seemed cluttered with packs delivered by the transport companies, thanks to which the pilgrims need carry no more than a little water for the day. I couldn't decide what to make of it.

At Bodenaya, I had also been warned that the number of pilgrims means that the competition hots up for a place at the inn (though that said, there are also more inns). To be on the safe side, it's simpler to phone ahead and reserve, which is what I did, and it turned out more or less all right. The contrast between two of the *albergues* in particular summed up, for me, the difference in atmosphere from everything I had experienced before.

Castañeda first of all. An unpretentious little bar-restaurant, with room for only a dozen people at most, clean and rudimentary: a bed to sleep in, a shower to wash in — what more does one need? People either sat inside to watch the football, or outside to chat and soothe their feet. The tables were set close together, which encourages conversation. The food was straightforward, but tasty and copious. The Way went past on the road, just in front of the terrace: pilgrims heading further along the Way passed by, and locals taking the air, or stopping in at the bar for a drink and a chat. From a little higher up the hill, behind the building, came the murmur of traffic on the highway; a reminder of the everyday life we will have to return to, and whose rhythm will no longer be that of walking along footpaths through imperturbable woods and eternal mountains. The sun sank slowly in the sky, the conversations petered out as the pilgrims, tired and full of food, went to their beds. I was one of the last to leave, the barman came out to offer me a drink and chew the fat; one of the advantages of walking alone is that these moments come to you more easily. It was simple, human, nothing else. I felt tired but at ease. I was nowhere in particular, but I was on my Way: the next day I would be walking again, I would end up somewhere else, what did it matter? Or perhaps, rather, that was what did matter.

I should really have avoided Santa Irene. Not that the *albergue* was ill kept, or dirty, or even disagreeable, quite the opposite. Doubtless others would have found it delightful. It was an old building, tastefully restored, with the old stone and wooden beams left visible, a shady little garden out the back, everything I like in fact. There was a sort of living-room with comfortable arm chairs, books on the shelves, I had the impression of being invited into somebody's house. Or rather, I had the impression that someone wanted to give that impression, and in the end it didn't quite come off. Rather like some of those bed and breakfasts where I've stayed in France, where the décor is supposed to look like the guest room, full of family clutter, except that it was all bought at a DIY shop and in the end it just feels fake. Then at table, the soup smelt too much of Knorr. It was too much like a holiday hotel for tourists, which is not what I was looking for. When all's said and done, I think I prefer the *albergue* Bela Muxía where I stayed later, on the coast at Muxía in fact. It was large, modern, built in concrete, everything was ultra-functional (At last! Showers designed by somebody who takes showers themselves and knows you need somewhere to hang your things without them getting wet!), but somehow it vibrated with the warmth of the welcome I got from the friendly couple at the desk, and their enthusiastic insistence that I should try their rooftop terrace giving an unequalled view of the town and the sea.

The closer I got to Santiago, the more people there seemed to be. Yet it still felt glorious to be up in the early morning when the air was fresh, and to start off down paths that wind among the eucalyptus trees; since Lugo, the weather had improved and by 11:00 it was already hot. Out of the woods, the hay was being gathered in, the air was full of the smell of cut grass, though the edges of the paths were still full of flowers.

I don't know if Santiago emits the effluvia of religion, but I felt the need for spiritual assistance, so to occupy my mind I set out to learn by heart Georges Brassens "Bad reputation", first in French and then in Paco Ibañez' Spanish version. Though after a while, I had to admit to myself that, however much the song may be a challenge to everything religious and moralising, it was singularly inappropriate to my circumstances. As I sang out loudly that "The good people don't like it when / you follow a different road from them", the fact is that I was following exactly the same road as thousands of others on their Way into Santiago at the rate, so I was told, of 1700 every day (and this wasn't even the high season). But whatever, thanks to Georges and Paco, it was gaily singing that I arrived on the heights that look down on the town of Compostela itself. Not even the sight of the immense, and immensely ugly, monument to Pope John-Paul II's pilgrimage to Compostela (I wonder if he carried his own back-pack) could dampen my high spirits. I followed the road that sloped steeply down towards the town, overtaking two young women one of whom seemed to have hurt her knee. I greeted them with the Way's habitual "Buen Camino", and walked on down.

I should have been used to it, but it is still a shame that the view pilgrims must once have had, of the walls of Santiago sheltering the cathedral within, their destination so long sought after and finally to hand, is now obscured by an agglomeration of roads, roundabouts, and buildings, in short by concrete and tarmac.

I entered the old town at last, down stone-paved streets empty of traffic, lined by handsome old buildings. I walked across the Praza Cervantes, with its solitary column topped by a bust of Spain's great author. Almost without seeing them, I walked through streets full of bars and shops selling souvenirs and other touristical and pilgrimistical knick-knacks. I passed under the archway leading into the great cathedral square, where two buskers played medieval bagpipe music that felt fitting to my mood and appropriate to the place. And there I was, at last, facing the cathedral, after three years and 1800km of walking. I sat down at the edge of the square and watched other pilgrims flowing in, some still with their backpacks and others who had clearly found their hostel already. The square was full of meetings, greetings, as little groups formed and broke up.

I had arrived alone, I had thought of going straight into the cathedral but backpacks are not permitted, and suddenly I felt at a loss. What should I do?

I had planned to stay two whole days in Compostela, in an *albergue* reserved in the town centre. I had intended to check in and leave my backpack before going off to see about obtaining my Compostela. But now that I had arrived, that didn't seem right. Without really understanding why, I felt a need for completion, to mark my arrival at the end of the Way there and then, by a definitive act. So I made my way from the square, not towards my *albergue*, but directly towards the *Oficina de Acollida ao Peregrino* or, less poetically, the Pilgrims' Reception.

About fifty pilgrims were queueing for their certificates. People chatted, the noise echoed, I seemed to be the only one not in a group and a wave of loneliness swept over me. I had no desire to talk, and I felt isolated, suspended in a temporal void, awaiting something. What exactly? I had no idea. To find what I had sought during all those kilometres, perhaps?

The dozen or so employees and volunteers at the Reception were efficient enough, and in the end, the queue moved forward quickly. I found myself facing a charming Irish lady who verified my *credential* and gave me my *Compostela*. I decided to fork out the princely sum of €3 for a personalised certificate, showing my starting point and the distance I had come (very precisely, 1763km); this was important, it will be framed and given to my granddaughter, maybe one day she will show it to her own grandchildren.

I decided not to buy the official cockleshell, marked with the St James' Cross. All along the Way, seeing pilgrims with the cockle on their packs had irritated me. In the old days, you were only allowed to carry the cockle once the pilgrimage was completed, to prove that you had accomplished your penance; the cockles were manufactured by a specialised guild, often in metal, and their sale was strictly controlled by the Church (for financial reasons as well, no doubt). Here then I could have rightfully displayed the cockle on my pack, yet all of a sudden the idea put me off. Confusedly, I had the feeling that a pilgrimage is worthless if it is not above all internal, and that to carry a visible sign would externalise it and somehow sterilise something that should remain internal and fecund. Instead, I went out into a little courtyard, where a fountain played gently into a basin.

I sat down again. I didn't know what to think. I was invaded by a sensation of anticlimax. Not disappointed, not in the least. But it was a bit as if I had expected the world to be different, and the world turned out to be just the same. Or that I would be different, only that I felt pretty much the same as the day before. Nothing comparable anyway, to that moment of exaltation in the Béarn when at last I saw the Pyrenees; or in the Basque Country when from the summit of a savage hill I spied the Atlantic; or on the path of *Los Ospedales* when the mountains were revealed behind the clouds.

As I left the *Acollida* I realised that I was happy; not euphoric, but happy. I walked under the rich hot sun, I went slowly back up the hill towards the Praza Cervantes to find my *albergue*, and more than anything a bar, for I was thirsty, and I had got into the habit of finishing the day with a *caña*, in other words a beer.

I found a bar with a few tables outside on the square. I sat down, then made room for a couple of Belgian pilgrims, the same age as myself. They were both short in stature, their faces tanned by the sun and lined by the wind, faces straight out of a Brueghel painting, especially since one of them wore a hat of vaguely medieval shape, with a cockle stuck to the front. We began chatting (of course!), a friendly cigarette was offered. I asked them why they walked the Way, and one replied "I'm retired, why should I bore myself stupid sitting at home? So I walk the Way". And he explained that he lived his life on the Camino. No sooner arrived in Compostela than he was off to the starting-point of another Spanish Camino.

Why not? It seemed to work for him. But not for me, I realised. In three days I planned to set out again, to follow the Way to the end of the Earth at Fisterra. Then, it would really be the end. After that, I needed to return, to find my own home, to mull over all that I have seen and felt, to understand at last, or so I hoped, what it was that I had found at the end of the Way.

Two days in Compostela

A strange feeling indeed, to wake up in the dormitory surrounded by the noise of parting pilgrims, without feeling the least involved. That day, I wasn't walking, I could take all the time I wanted.

I was staying in the *albergue* "El Ultimo Scello", partly because it is in the city centre close to the Praza Cervantes, but partly also because according to my guide it was next door to the best *chocolate con churros* of all Compostela. Moved by an ever alert culinary curiosity, I had first tasted the recipe in Comillas and it had been a revelation, almost a mystical experience (you will have noticed that I'm fond of chocolate). I had never tasted anything like it: the hot chocolate is so thick that it must be stirred constantly if it is not to solidify, in a special container with an arm that turns unceasingly, moving through the thick and unctuous liquid. It is so thick that I found it hard to decide whether I should use the spoon to stir it, or to eat it like a soup. The *churro* is basically a long thin doughnut, served hot and sprinkled with sugar, which you dunk in the chocolate. Normally I don't like dunking, neither biscuits in tea nor croissants in coffee, but I have to admit that this is something different; a croissant dunked in coffee becomes soggy and formless, leaving crumbs floating in the cup, whereas the *churro* comes out trailing royal robes of chocolate, leaving not a trace of its passing in the smooth and imperturbable surface of the *chocolate*.

My first destination in Compostela was therefore obvious: all I had to do was to cross the doorway of the *albergue* to find myself at the counter where this morning elixir is served. The café was run by a taciturn woman in her fifties, with a somewhat masculine air about her, with short cut hair and a strong chin, dressed in jeans and a shirt with a collar. My antennae were barely awake, but little by little the friendly atmosphere of the place worked its magic; most of the customers were clearly regulars on their way to work, many of them women alone or in groups, who greeted the lady at the bar like an old acquaintance. I felt at home there, and the home-made *chocolate* was indeed excellent. In the days that followed I became a regular myself, and on my return from Fisterra I was greeted with a triumphal "high five" to celebrate the completion of my Way's last stage.

What was I to do here in Compostela, my three years' destination? I had often heard tell of the *botafumeiro*, the famous thurible where incense is burned during Mass, suspended from the cathedral roof and so heavy it needs a team of muscular men to swing it the whole length of the nave. I suppose that in the Middle Ages, the incense was burned not just for ceremonial reasons but to cover the smell of the thousands of pilgrims come to hear Mass, and who had travelled so far without the benefit of the daily shower that every *albergue* offers us, their 21st century successors; sometimes they even slept and ate on the floor of the cathedral. The trouble is that to see the thurible in action you must go to Mass, and since I had been blessed already in Laredo I felt I had already paid my dues on that score.

Nonetheless, one should see the cathedral and so I set out, fortified by the comforting taste of *chocolate* sticking to my mouth.

You enter by way of the great square, the Praza do Obradoiro. With the best will in the world, I found it hard to feel any empathetic vibrations from the cathedral's façade. The enormous baroque entrance, covered with useless embellishments piled one on top of the other, is flanked on each side by heavy, even oppressive buildings whose straight lines and squares are more reminiscent of a fortress or worse still a prison, than of a structure aspiring to lift itself to the glory of God. I found the interior more evocative: it is the largest Romanesque church in Spain, and one of the largest in Europe (sadly, I was unable to see the Portico de la Gloria which was under restoration). The purity and simplicity of its outline reminded me of Vézelay where my pilgrimage had begun, the sunshine filtered through small windows placed high in the walls creating a half-light propitious for meditation. I would have found it much more evocative had it not been for the enormous altarpiece covered in gold that surrounds a 13th century statue of St James. I was reminded of a conversation on the Way near Lugo with a Californian born into a poor Mexican family and who told me how even her devout father would fulminate against the Church's ostentatious display of wealth in the midst of a poverty-stricken population.

I walked round by the ambulatory where I found a Mass in progress, in French, in one of the little side chapels. A group of about thirty francophone faithful was there to listen; it was the first time on the Way that I had seen so many people gathered together for an avowedly religious purpose — hardly surprising I suppose, given the place. I lit a candle for the couple who ran the campsite at Ascain in the Basque Country, and who had refused, the previous year, to take any money from a pilgrim; later, I would send them a postcard to let them know I had fulfilled my promise. Then I lit another for my ex-wife, deceased in 2015. At the end, we could no longer tolerate each other, the divorce was painful and conflictual for both of us; "peace be on her soul", I said to myself. Why was I doing this, why was I making this meaningless gesture, meaningless anyway for the unbeliever that I am. A last sacrifice to the centuries of belief that founded that European culture whose child I am, despite everything? Or was it rather in the hope of finding peace in my own soul, still haunted by the woman with whom I shared 20 years of my existence? My mind went back to the tiny hamlet of St Goussaud that I had passed through the year before, in France. There was a "lantern of the dead" outside the cemetery where it was the custom to light a flame whenever there was a burial, to make sure that the soul of the defunct could find its way and did not stay behind to trouble the living. I understood then the psychological value of these practices hidden beneath the mask of religious belief. They concern not the dead, who are no longer there to be troubled by them, but the living still inhabited by the dead, whose weight they must lay down for the sake of their own mental health.

I was disappointed by the candles. Today, they are everywhere electric. You drop your coin in a slot, and a little electronic candle lights up; the manual gesture that once picked the candle from a wooden box, feeling the wax yield slightly to the fingers' pressure, then carefully lit the little flame, no longer has any meaning; everything is reduced to its simplest expression, that is to say, money.

In fact it's all over the cathedral. You go up a narrow little staircase behind the statue of St James where the faithful bend to kiss the back of his neck (I didn't), and there's a box to drop your money in; go down to the crypt to admire the goldsmith's craft on the reliquary supposed to contain the saint's bones and there's another box for your money; in front of every statue proposed for the adoration of believers, a money box, in every chapel dedicated to this or that saint, money box after money box held out for holy offerings. I took to my heels.

Undeterred, I crossed the Praza da Quintana de Mortos to visit the church and museum of the Benedictine monastery of San Martiño Pinario (I'm always up for a museum).

Passing through rooms that were still being laid out, I found myself in the 17th century church, built 500 years after the cathedral. It confirmed an impression that had been growing in me ever since my departure from Bilbao: religious architecture in Spain (or at least in its northern provinces) has remained faithful to the Romanesque style, merely adding to it a superficial baroque decoration. A subjective impression no doubt, but it is as if the architects of the 12th century struggled with the limits of their art to rise towards God, whereas those of the 17th century contented themselves with copying their predecessors by pure conservatism. Nowhere had I encountered that evolution towards the Gothic that you find in Northern Europe, sprung from an aspiration towards light and lightness made stone, one of whose finest examples is Gloucester Cathedral in England, with its immense East window springing into air, whose pillars seem barely substantial enough to stand alone. It must be partly due to the climate: letting light flood into a church would not have the same effect in the heat of a Spanish summer as it does several hundred kilometres to the north. But only partly, I suspect. Don't forget that in the North, the High Middle Ages also witnessed the emergence of commercial towns, guilds, industries, and all the humanist thought that went with them. Nothing like that happened in Spain. First, there was the monstrous catastrophe of the Reconquista and the persecution of Jews and Muslims that followed, destroying the most skilful communities of merchants, artisans, and intellectuals, and cutting the ties of trade with the Mediterranean. That disaster was followed by another, disguised as a godsend: the discovery of the Americas and above all, of the Peruvian silver mines whose enormous production allowed the Spanish monarchy to avoid any concessions towards a moneyed commercial class which was only getting to its feet with difficulty. The Spanish monarchy and aristocracy thus became the most fervent and the most reactionary defenders of the Catholic Church for centuries to come: it is no accident that the abominable Holy Inquisition first appeared in Spain.

One might object that Italy did not experience any fundamental change in its architectural forms either, especially not the northern evolution towards the Gothic style, and that its churches also have remained solidly anchored in the Romanesque. That's true of course (and the same climatic factors may have played a role there). But paradoxically, despite the presence of the Pope in Rome, Italy was never subjected to such an absolute power of the Church. On the contrary the flourishing of the Renaissance in Italy was the period of flourishing cities, with their commerce and industry, each of them proudly asserting its independence against both the nobility and the Church's temporal power. I find it hard to imagine Pisa's Campo Santo in Spain, with its stunning apotheosis of white, green and red marble vaunting to the world the wealth, splendour, and pride of its citizens; or the frescoes of San Frediano in Lucca full of brutal caricatures of their patrons' own venality; or even the joyful, lighthearted Sicilian baroque.

In Spain there was never a Reformation, only ever a Counter-Reformation.

The masterpiece of the church of San Martiño is to be found in the choir, and in the enormous altarpiece which faces out into the nave, and in, towards the choir. The whole is a rich profusion of sculpture in wood by Mateo de Prado. The figures in the choir are admirably rendered, full of life and emotion, but while I can admire the artistic skill I confess that the emotion leaves me cold: too much sentimentality and not enough sensitivity.

The altarpiece is an extraordinary achievement of wood and gilt, rising towards the ceiling with an airy lightness that far surpasses the similar works I have seen elsewhere. But still, it feels much more like a display of wealth to the glory of the Benedictine order and its aristocratic benefactors than a devotional work: far removed indeed from the austere simplicity of Cistercian abbeys like Thoronet, conceived as instruments of music to amplify the voices of monks lifting upwards to the Heavens, and bare of any decoration which might distract the soul in search of the sublime.

How are we to explain such contrasts? The origins of the Catholic Church are to be found in the adoption of Christianity as the official religion of Roman imperial power, under Constantine. Ever since, it has constantly tried to find an impossible equilibrium between the egalitarian, even communist thought of Christ, which not even the clean-up of the Gospels during the 4th century has been able to expunge completely from the Bible, and the imperial demand that it should impose itself on the population through its ostentatious wealth and temporal power. This is why all the religious movements which tried to return to Christ's original message by seeking support among the poor and the exploited, constantly ran the risk of excommunication. St Francis himself was nearly condemned for heresy, and not just any heresy: he had preached the doctrine of Christ's poverty. The English priest and philosopher John Wycliffe, who was the first to translate the Bible into English so that it should be accessible to the people, was excommunicated after his death, his bones burned and their ashes thrown into the river.

When we come to the Counter-Reformation, everything that had been revolutionary in Christian thought fled the Church for the various protestant sects: the Quakers, Thomas Münzer's Anabaptists, the Levellers of the English Revolution, and many others. In Spain the Church was left with the power of the rich and of a henceforth utterly reactionary social order, matched by a morbid religiosity which I find reflected in much of El Greco's work, however much I admire the talent of the artist himself.

My thoughts wandered back to the Way, and a Spanish fellow *caminero* to whom I had complained one day about the impossibility of visiting most churches. "How is it", I asked him, "that in Spain, this most Catholic of European countries, the churches are always locked?". His reply gave me food for thought: "Don't forget that it's also in Spain that the most churches have been burned down". Especially in the Asturias. In 1934, a revolt of Asturian miners took power briefly in the town of Oviedo; to put down the revolt, the republican government very democratically called on an officer who was to become famous, or infamous, shortly after — General Franco. By a singular irony of history, this representative of the Spanish right, for which the Reconquista has always been a favourite symbol, did not hesitate to call in Muslim moorish troops to "reconquer" the only part of Spain which had never fallen under Muslim rule. Hardly surprising then, that I found perfectly sinister the paintings displayed in the rooms of San Martiño, of the great men of this reactionary church, and that it was with a feeling of relief that I walked from religious obscurity into the light of a sun whose brilliance owes nothing to God and everything to the forces of nature and physics.

I set off in search of a bar to quench my thirst and to get rid of the religious gloom. On the other side of the square, I spied a little group sitting around a table and discovered to my delight my German friends from Bodenaya. Warm were our greetings, and lively the conversation, then little by little the group dissolved until there were only two of us left, myself and a German in his fifties walking the Way in memory of a child deceased. We spent five hours together, talking of the Way and of life, and when we finally went our separate ways, I found myself deeply moved by this expression of the solidarity of the Way, and still more, honoured by the confidence that had been placed in me.

Evening fell, by chance in the Praza das Praterías next to the cathedral I came across a brass band concert, of Spanish music for the most part. The broad staircase leading up to the cathedral was densely packed, people sat there in silence, subjugated like me by the music. Slowly, the sun descended lower in the sky, its light became softer, caressing the buildings whose old stone shone with those rich and luminous yellows so characteristic of limestone. The music told me its tales of those harsh landscapes, baked by the sun, and of the people of Spain who perhaps, in the bottom of their hearts, are more Sancho Panza than Don Quixote. As night fell, the concert came to an end and I went off to find my supper, in a modest little café under the sign of the great Cervantes.

I began the next day by ambling through the pleasant streets of the old town: there are colonnades to protect walkers from the sun, the cafés are full of animated discussion, you can happily get lost there. I strolled down to the Abastos, the old covered market, where I drank a glass of chilled white wine surrounded by stalls full of cherries as big as plums, spicy chorizos hanging in bunches, cheese, bread, everything to entice you into the innocent pleasures of the flesh.

I decided to visit the Pilgrimage Museum. It's a fine museum, recently built and instructive without being ponderous. I learnt more of the importance of the pilgrimage to Compostela in medieval history, not just from the spiritual or ideological standpoint but still more economically. Many towns, especially on the Camino Francés, owe their growth or even their existence to the money earned from passing pilgrims. Even more than the money, the travelling pilgrims, the artisans called to build the churches and the *ospedales*, and the doctors who cared for the pilgrims' injuries and sicknesses, helped to spread skills and knowledge throughout Spain, and even throughout Europe (hence the arabesques that I had admired the previous year at the church of Bénévent l'Abbaye). The exhibition spoke of the phenomenon of pilgrimage in general, throughout the world. Why? I asked myself, not for the first time: what was it that pushed so many men and women, over the centuries and all over the planet, to wander in search of something, a meaning, that they couldn't find at home? And when we see the crowds of tourists from every country imaginable wandering through the Paris Louvre, in a certain sense are they not also pilgrims? Once at the Louvre, plunged in contemplation of a work by Leonardo da Vinci, lost in thought, I found myself surrounded by a group of middle-aged Chinese tourists accompanied by a guide who explained the picture to them. They talked, they took photos, as if I wasn't there. It could have irritated me, but on the contrary

I was touched. These people had travelled thousands of kilometres to come here, they could have gone to Disneyland or the Galeries Lafayette, but they were here, pondering a painting that must be every bit as opaque for them as Chinese painting is for me. And on their return to China, they would take with them a small piece of understanding from another culture, and the world will be a little less divided into nations that are strangers to each other.

In the museum you also discover the story of Santiago Matamoros, or how St James became a "Killer of Moors", by appearing mystically to lead an outnumbered Christian army to victory against the Moors at the Battle of Clavijo — a battle, appropriately enough, that in reality never took place. Poor old James! You were a modest man, a cousin and disciple of Christ who set out to preach love for our fellow man in a world without rich and poor, without exploitation, what would you have said to find yourself transformed into the emblem of the Reconquista, of the hatred, violence, and obscurantism of an aristocratic caste that emptied Spain of its Arab and Jewish populations? The Reconquista was barely done, but they took you with them beyond the Azores, to the other side of the Atlantic, to make you "Santiago Mataindios", "Killer of Indians". Then, by one of those ironies of which history is so fond, you were recuperated by a few rebel Indians to become "Santiago Matahispanos", "Killer of Spaniards". I assure you James, my poor old friend, I didn't come to Compostela to see you hoisted on a heap of corpses, covered in gold, silver, and futile ornament, mummified in your baroque sanctuary. I came for something else entirely. What? Did I find it in the end? I couldn't say.

Among the exhibits, I noticed a Japanese scroll. It's a sort of *credential* for the pilgrimage to visit the 88 buddhist temples founded by the monk Kobo Daichi on the island of Shikoku in Japan, 1200km walking on the other side of the planet, in a country that you, James, had never heard of or even imagined. It gave me an idea…

Leaving the museum, I returned to the cathedral in search of calm and shade. All of a sudden I found myself face to face with the young woman with the injured knee whom I had greeted on my way down into Compostela. To my surprise she recognised me also, and I was struck once again by the way pilgrims recognise each other in a crowd after even the most fleeting encounters. We began one of those conversations that start so easily in our international fraternity; she was Mexican, only 20 years old, travelling alone, I thought her very brave. It came to me that she really was a very pretty woman, jet-black hair cut short, flashing black eyes, delicate features, a gentle and intelligent expression, a graceful, willowy body. We shared the same unease before so much ostentatious wealth, and we left the cathedral together to walk up towards the Praza Cervantes. She had not much time, she was leaving the city, but for a short moment we found mutual pleasure in each other's company. We were taking our leave with the usual civilities, under the gaze of Cervantes on his column, when all of a sudden she seized me by the arms and kissed me on both cheeks; then she turned on her heels and walked off with a quick and confident step, to disappear into the crowd and, no doubt, for ever from my life. I just stood there, dumbstruck. What on Earth just happened? I really had no idea, I certainly hadn't seen it coming.

Two days later at the *albergue* in Santa Mariña on the Camino de Fisterra, I was to strike up a conversation with an American five years my elder. I had the feeling I had seen him somewhere before, but I couldn't place him. Then suddenly it came to me: he could have been the twin brother of Proctor & Gamble's Mister Clean.

The conversation was interesting, as it nearly always is with Americans whose culture is so different and foreign to our own, but I was increasingly ill at ease when he went on at what seemed to me unnecessary length about his encounters on the Way with young women who had found him "interesting" (no other word seems to fit the bill). He had never had any actual adventures of course. But then my Mexican acquaintance and her brief gesture came back to me, followed by others: that young woman from Madrid for example, whom I had met in Irun and then encountered again by chance at a café in San Sebastián where I had stopped for breakfast, we had spend an agreeable day walking and talking together. It made me wonder — though I said nothing — whether Mister Clean had not got the wrong end of the stick entirely. Is it not the difference in age that removes all ambiguity from the encounter, and that makes it possible for a young woman to start a conversation freely with a man, without having to be on her guard for unwanted attentions? To be, however briefly and in however limited a way, no longer a woman on her guard with a man, but simply a human being in the company of another? That seemed to me not impossible, especially when I turned the configuration the other way around: I remember my pleasure in Irun at finding myself in an *albergue* full of young people and to feel that I was not an "old man", or worse still a "senior citizen", expected to limit myself to the senior citizen's concerns, but just another human being with whom it was possible to share and to talk. So goes the fraternity of the Way.

All these thoughts came to me later. For the moment, I returned to the "Ultimo Scello", troubled and perplexed. In the common room I tried to return to my writing, but the words wouldn't come. The afternoon drew to a close and dusk filled the room. A sound of music, of jazz, filtered in from the street. I went out to look for it.

In the Praza de Feixóo, 50m away, a jazz trio played in front of the church (Compostela is full of churches). The square was crammed, people sat on the ground chatting, children ran around and danced; no pilgrims, I thought, more like locals.

The sky grew darker, the town lights sparkled more brightly. All around me people were chatting, engaged in animated discussion, laughing… I was filled with melancholy. I longed for a friend, or a group of friends, or better still a partner. But there was nobody, and I

didn't feel up to starting a conversation with a chance neighbour, especially not in Spanish. I went off to bed; the next day, after some
hesitation, I had decided to head on to Fisterra and the ends of the
Earth.

The ends of the Earth

At Santiago, you have a choice: either conclude your pilgrimage at Compostela, or take to the Way again and walk to Fisterra (sometimes called Finisterra), the ends of the Earth, which claims to be the westernmost point of the Eurasian continent. For a long time, I couldn't imagine going any further than Santiago, it seemed so far off and out of reach. But now that I had arrived, after two days I was already missing the feel of the Way under my feet, I wanted to see the sea again, and to push on to where the land comes to an end.

I remembered a science-fiction novel I had read many years ago, whose title and author I have completely forgotten, but whose story resurges in my mind from time to time. It tells of a city mounted on an enormous tractor, obliged to make its way without stopping across the planet, for the planet itself is of a weird shape, constantly created in front of the city and disappearing into the void behind it. To escape the void, the city must build its own road across unknown terrain, traversing mountains, rivers, lakes… In the end, you realise that the planet is none other than Earth after some unspecified societal collapse, and that its strange form and progressive dissolution are mental illusions generated in the minds of the city's inhabitants by its own experimental power station. The story begins as the city, after generations spent crossing the entire Eurasian continent from China, is confronted with the Atlantic Ocean and its navigators try vainly to build a bridge to reach the other side of this "lake" whose far shore they cannot even see. If this story sprang to my mind unbidden once again, perhaps it is to express my own need to confront this ultimate shore where it is impossible to go further, where the only choice left is to call into question everything that up to then had seemed solid and certain. And so, to begin again, to take up life anew but from another angle.

On the coast there are two destinations: Fisterra itself, and Muxía. The tradition is to follow the Way as far as Hospital, then turn towards Fisterra, after which you go north for 30km along the coast until you arrive at Muxía. For reasons which were never very clear, I decided to go to Muxía first, and then walk down towards Fisterra. Maybe I wanted to get away from the promiscuity of the last few days, and to take to a Way which promised to be less frequented, or so I hoped.

Whatever, here I was once again on the Way, by a fine sunny morning which promised to be hot later. The eucalyptus forests in the hills around Compostela gave way to a broad plain and its extensive farms.

A fine Roman bridge crosses the river at Ponte Maceira. In midsummer the river was far from full, but its clear water flowed noisily over the rocks and between flourishing tufts of white flowers. It was hot, I was sweating, the river seemed to open its arms to invite me to plunge into its refreshing waters. Why didn't I accept the invitation? I wasn't in a hurry, I had the whole day before me. Hard to explain, but walking takes me like that, as if a magnet at the end of the road pulled me irresistibly onwards. Perhaps too, more prosaically, it's just that I know it will be harder to stop and start again than to press on. When I think about it, I realise that I only stopped once to swim along the Way, in the chill waters of the river at Sauveterre-en-Béarn, and when I reread these lines they sound to me more like a rationalisation than a reason, a rational reason but one that doesn't get to the bottom of things.

So I went on, and crossed the river. The heat of the sun reverberated from the stone, but was softened by the fresh air rising from the river. Opposite, a little chapel in the Spanish style: square, austere, decorated with a coat of arms over the door and a small, vaguely baroque, open bell tower, again the same disconcerting mixture of solidity and flourish.

Shortly after I arrived at Negreira, an almost obligatory stopping point given the distance to the next one. At first sight it is not a very interesting town, it is even a bit depressing: concrete, dust, heat, the streets almost empty, more or less recent buildings surrounded by scrubby patches of vegetation. The *albergue* is in a modern apartment block, right at the end of a street leading towards the town centre in a desperately straight line; the intended shop-fronts were all walled up, victims or so I suppose of the collapse of the wave of speculative building that swept over Spain before the crisis of 2007. Inside it was noisy, the concrete walls echoing with the chatter of adolescents who had occupied the spaces along with their monitors. An attractive bunch of youngsters on the whole. And then, there was a big garden with benches and chairs, where it felt good to sit down to read, and to put together a few notes of the day.

I wandered into town looking for somewhere to eat, and came across a café-restaurant with an evening menu that tempted me. I was in that odd state of mind where I didn't feel like talking to anyone but neither did I feel like being alone. I wanted to be surrounded by people, and the café, filling up with its clearly local customers, suited me admirably. On the terrace, a couple of large TV screens were installed, that evening there would be a World Cup match between Spain and Iran, a real match of David and Goliath. I don't follow football at all, but just for once I felt like watching a match: I liked the idea of watching Spain play surrounded by Spaniards (even if they were Galicians), and I have had a soft spot for the Iranians ever since I worked there many years ago. I would love to see them win, however unlikely that seemed.

In the end it was a good match. The Iranians didn't win of course, but they played very well. Around me, the Spanish audience followed the match with enthusiasm but without the hysterical nationalist effluvium that so often emanates from supporters. And to top it off, I ate well.

It was not until dawn the next day, on my way out of the town, that I discovered Negreira's most interesting aspect. An old street of little shops, all in stone, led down towards a gate in the town wall. In the street, I was confronted by a strange bronze statue, of a visibly poor man setting out with a determined stride, except that his feet were transformed into roots planted in his native soil. From an opening in the wall behind him leaned a child, his son no doubt, crying for him to return, and on the other side of the wall a woman sat, holding a baby on her knees. The whole thing was crowned by a globe of the world, but I could see no inscription, nothing to indicate the subject, nor the artist, nor the date. What could it be? It seemed to be a monument to the sorrow of emigration, the forced emigration of the poor, who must have been so many to leave this region of Spain. But who had it made, and why? Even Mr Google had no explanation.

•••

Logoso is an attractive hamlet where you arrive along a dirt track, and which is barely accessible for motor vehicles. You can swim in the nearby river, but I only discovered this the next morning on my way out. The little *albergue* is charming and the food excellent.

I had an experience there which could have turned awkward or even unpleasant. Following my usual routine I had showered on arriving, exchanged a few words with a Japanese couple already settled in the dormitory, and then fallen asleep. I was still in that fragile space

180

between two worlds, when my hesitant awakening was jostled by the noisy arrival of a French group. There were four of them, in their sixties, and they were settling in as if the dormitory belonged to them, talking loudly and without taking the least notice of anybody else.

In such circumstances, one is easily bad-tempered. I got out of the bed and told them off roundly: "You there, the French abroad with your bad manners, that's enough of it…". Total astonishment on their part: they really hadn't expected to be aggressed like that, and in French with an English accent to top it all. A certain mutual embarrassent set in, one of them apologised politely enough, I accepted it, and peace returned.

When I awoke completely, the Frenchmen were no longer in the dormitory and it occurred to me that the situation was not entirely comfortable. I didn't regret the gesture, it seemed to me necessary to react, but maybe I had overdone it a bit, and now we all had to get along somehow in this very small *albergue*. What to do?

I went out into the street and up to the bar of the *albergue*, where I found my group of Frenchmen settled at a table. It was time for a quiet beer, to relax and to chew the fat before the evening meal.

I apologised for my own bad temper, I went the round of the table shaking hands with everyone, they apologised again, and invited me to take a seat. A moment of hesitation, and I accepted… And in fact they turned out to be amiable enough, and for the first time I met with a group of real Catholics on pilgrimage. Not that it showed too much! We drank, we ate, we joked, the evening wiled away in the game of wit and banter that the French enjoy so much, and that I have always enjoyed. Still, I could feel we had nothing but our humanity in common, and that this was not an encounter I particularly wanted to prolong. To tell the truth I was somewhat relieved at the idea that the next day I would take the turning off to Muxía and would probably be alone again on the Way.

I wondered why people behave like that abroad (and not just the French either, it has to be said that neither the British nor the Germans have a very good reputation in this respect). I was reminded of the groups of adolescents I sometimes see in the streets of my Parisian suburb, who laugh, and shout, and occupy the space… I've often thought that fundamentally, they feel unsure of themselves. When you're an adolescent you're entering into the adult world, a world that belongs to adults, but you've still not completely arrived, nor are you entirely sure there's room for you. The feeling is all the stronger in that the space is already occupied by the older generations. So you have to make space, oblige the adult world to make room for you, by pushing and shoving a bit, so to speak. And when people are abroad, especially when they don't speak the local language, they experience an analogous sensation of insecurity. Talking loud, imposing yourselves as a group, creating a group walled against the uncertainty emanating from the otherness of the foreigner, all that is reassuring; it's a cut-price reassurance, but a reassurance just the same.

I set off at dawn the next morning, expecting a long hot day. The sun was barely visible in a sky just barely blue. The wind turbines stretched off gracefully towards the horizon.

Shortly before Muxía I met up with an Australian of my own age, who had been walking for the last several days with a young German in her thirties. I had met them two days earlier in San Mariña, they seemed to have developed one of those camaraderies that spring up along the Way, from meetings repeated evening after evening. Strange companions on the Way, I had thought, who seemed at first sight to have nothing in common; stranger still in that both seemed thin-skinned and not very at ease with other people. Yet they seemed to get on well enough together, and that was the main thing. Who am I to judge after all, and indeed, why should I even want to?

That day, they were walking with the Australian art restorer in her thirties, whom I mentioned earlier. She was specialised in contemporary art but had done her thesis on the specific problems of restoring aboriginal art. An unusual trade, I thought to myself, about which I know nothing. I always find it interesting when people recount their trade or their passion. When you step outside your own usual centres of interest, you always learn something, so I seized the chance to question her. And indeed, I learned something of the complexity of aboriginal technique, the difficulty of producing from purely natural, unworked materials, a surface smooth and flat enough to take and retain colour, colours that adhere to the surface and that don't lose their initial hue or tone.

So we arrived together in Muxía, which turned out to be a pleasant little fishing port, whose narrow streets built in old stone squeeze together in the narrow confines of a promontory that juts out like a finger into the ocean. We each went our separate ways towards our hostels, promising to meet again for the evening meal.

At the end of the promontory is the church dedicated to St Mary, who is supposed to have landed here to help St James bring the good word to the Iberians, and I directed my steps towards this miraculous place. Triply miraculous in fact, for not only is the presence here of Saints James and Mary highly unlikely, not to say unbelievable, but the Virgin is supposed to have pushed the miraculous to the point of sailing in a stone boat, proof of the miracle if ever you needed one. And the proof is there, scattered on the ocean's edge: massive stones with strange vaguely boat-like shapes, sculpted and rounded by millennia of waves, winds, and bad weather.

The best of the story is that these stones with their disconcerting shapes were worshipped long before the arrival of Christianity. Yet again, the Church has hijacked for its own benefit the centuries, if not millennia of belief that preceded it. And I wondered if I had not arrived, here in Muxía, at the real end of the Way, at an object of pilgrimage far older than Compostela. And if here I were not walking in the steps not just of my medieval ancestors, but of elders more ancient still. Did they worship the same gods here as they did at Carnac or Stonehenge?

That evening was the night of St John, traditionally marked by bonfires and a night of celebration. After eating, our little group went off in search of fire and fiesta, but we found none. Instead, nothing but this deserted beach where the sun plunged into the sea so slowly it was hypnotic, in a light like the world's end. Beyond, an ocean of dreams, of hope, of melancholy.

I agreed with my friendly art restorer to set off together the next day, and to walk half the way to Fisterra. She planned to go all the way, but I was on vacation so to speak, and I had given myself two whole days to walk the 30km between Muxía and Fisterra. As if I really didn't want to stop walking.

I took the opportunity to ask her something about modern aboriginal art. The little I had seen up to then, in Australian showrooms especially, had always left me feeling ambivalent, not to say unconvinced. In itself, I found it beautiful: looking at a painting there is no doubt that we stand before a true work of art which is part of our common human heritage. This can often be frustrating: we find ourselves in the presence of work full of signs and significance for those who created it, and for the audience to which it is destined, but not for us, just as the interior of a cathedral must be incomprehensible to those who know nothing of the Christian tradition. But what bothers me most is that the culture which gave birth to the painting is dead or moribund, brutally swept away by British colonialism, then by industrialisation and modernity. The aboriginal Australians are parked in reserves, their lands and the lands of their ancestors were stolen from them, first by the farmers and then by the mining companies, they are confronted by the endemic racism of Australian society and subject to all the scourges of poverty, of which alcoholism is only one. To paint in the old tradition, isn't that running the risk of merely reproducing old themes whose real life is no longer anchored in the vitality of a living society? Or else, is the artist not condemned to stay cloistered within the confines of an "indigenous" idiom from which he is forbidden to escape?

As always, things are not that simple. Some time later, I met an Australian artist who knew well an outback aboriginal art workshop, and he showed me pictures that changed my outlook. Obviously, in a place like that there are pieces destined for sale to the tourists — but any artist has to sell his production and is therefore obliged, at least up to a point, to submit to current taste. But there were other very original pieces, which allied the techniques and the lively sense of colour and form that are found in the traditional art, with themes, in particular landscapes that are recognisable for us. Today's aboriginal artists have also freed themselves from the constraints imposed by the natural materials they once used, and have cheerfully adopted acrylics. Finally, and this is not the least important aspect, many of them are women who free themselves, through art and the income it has generated, from dependence on the patriarchal norms in their traditional society.

My Australian friend left me at Lires, and the following day I walked gently through the last kilometres that took me into Fisterra.

A funny town, Fisterra. I couldn't decide whether I liked it or not. There's a side to it like a rundown seaside resort, with a seafront disfigured by bars and restaurants with no particular character. But I was won over, little by little, by a certain nostalgic charm to the place. First, there's the fact that this is still an active fishing port with all its working life of ship chandlers, small ship repair yards, cables, fishing nets, everything that makes a sort of no-man's land joining land and sea, somewhere between the world of people and the world of dolphins, fish, and mermaids… Then as you walk up from the port into the town, you quickly get lost in a labyrinth of old streets where it is easy to see in your mind's eye, strolling groups of fishermen and fishwives dressed in clogs and long blue skirts.

It has an eccentric side too, that you meet on the way into town from Muxía: a house decorated with all kinds of odds and ends reminiscent of the sea or the Camino, a sort of miniature Palais du Facteur Cheval. Then there's the Café La Frontera, a welcoming place where you can eat vegetarian/vegan as well as the usual tapas, and which proposes next door a clothes shop advertising "Hippie / chillout / Goa fashion".

Fisterra seems indeed to be something of a 'hippie refuge", as if the hippies had arrived here, at the ends of the Earth, and being unable to go any further, had simply sat down here and stayed. There are several *albergues* in a style decidedly influenced by "peace and love", and I ended up in one of them more or less by accident. I found the atmosphere very odd, with a strong aftertaste of my younger days, of my twenties full of dreams and illusions when I too dressed in coloured Indian shirts and bell-bottom trousers. It was almost unnerving to find myself surrounded by youngsters so much like the youngster I once was, so many years ago now.

At the *albergue* I was, much against my will, witness to a scene which reminded me why I had never been entirely convinced by the ideology of "peace and love". In a room whose door was inscribed "love is everywhere", the person in charge of the *albergue* was engaged in a dispute with one of the volunteers over some business of money and responsibilities. I didn't understand everything, nor did I want to. At least in an ordinary company, HR doesn't deal with this kind of issue in public, still less in front of the "customer". Here though, "love" and "openmindedness" mean that everything has to be out in the open, and it left a bad taste in my mouth. This is why "peace and love" never works, in the end, especially not in the world we live in: it is humanly impossible to love everybody all the time, except perhaps for the saints, and not even then. It's like happiness: if you were never unhappy, how would you know what it is?

I left peace and love behind me, and set off towards the lighthouse; the ultimate end of the Earth. There was nobody else on the path along the cliffs, passing through woods and over heather-flowered moorland. Before reaching the lighthouse I stopped, sat down on a rock, and let my gaze lose itself in the sea spread out to infinity before me, peaceful, merging into the clouds on the horizon. The ocean was featureless, my mind blank with melancholy. Everything here would end, definitively. Where should I go next? What should I do with my life? If life is a journey, can we journey aimlessly, and if not, then what aim should we fix ourselves? That is the peril of the Way, it sets you before these questions and then leaves you there, before an ephemeral and transient horizon, without any answer.

The Way back

I took the bus back to Compostela from Fisterra, then the train towards home. The train passed through León and crossed the Meseta, which is where the Camino Francés goes. Looking out of the window at this immense plain, burned by the sun, I said to myself that the Camino Francés must be every bit as taxing as the Norte I have just walked. Suddenly the Way stretched out before me again, I began to think of setting off again, as soon as possible, next year why not: this time, I would start from Paris and walk the whole Way along the Camino Francés, I would confront the challenge of the Meseta.

But why seek a challenge? That was not why I had undertaken the pilgrimage, like so many I set out in search of something, even if I did not know clearly what I was looking for, even if the object of my quest changed along the thread of kilometres. Perhaps it has something to do with the sight of all those backpacks delivered at the entrances to the *albergues*. I realised that this way of doing things was not for me, that I needed to put myself to the test both physically and mentally. It was a reasonable challenge, after all Compostela is hardly the North Pole, but a challenge nonetheless. And yet again, I ask myself, why? In olden days, pilgrims imposed such challenges, and much worse, on themselves, out of penitence, seeking through pain the forgiveness of their sins. But I didn't feel any need for forgiveness, and who would forgive me anyway? It's certain that you don't walk life's Way without committing faults, even if they are only sins against your own conception of what is right; like anybody else, I have enough to reproach myself with. I know that I have made others suffer out of stupidity, or thoughtlessness, or self-centredness, or lack of empathy rather than outright malice, at least so I hope. But from there to do penance… it goes against the grain of everything I have believed in for many a year. Long ago, wanting to improve my French, I undertook to read André Malraux's *La condition humaine.* I didn't understand it very well, but one scene remained etched in my memory. One of the novel's characters declares: once you are out of adolescence, then having regrets only means being unable to learn from experience. As a young man, that struck me as profoundly true, and I tried to live by it thereafter. Guilt that imprisons you in the past prevents you from improving and so growing. This is why it is also possible to wallow in guilt. It may seem paradoxical, but guilt can also allow you to avoid taking responsibility for your actions: the feeling of guilt is penance that dispenses you from learning and changing.

Never to feel guilt is the mark of the sociopath. To wallow in guilt is a sort of perverse indulgence.

Then there are moments when we do things which make others suffer, but which are necessary if we are to remain true to ourselves, or simply to survive emotionally and psychologically. When I left my wife — for I was indeed the one who took the initiative — I caused her terrible suffering, I cannot hide from it, and I was ill with guilt. But our relationship had reached a point where for me, my psychological survival was at stake. We have a right to defend ourselves: should I feel guilty as a consequence?

No penance then, but a challenge is something else. Increasingly, it seems to me that nothing worth doing or living comes easily, without effort. I feel as if I have only really learned this late in life, I should have understood it long ago. There are surely reasons for that. First of all, to be a worker (or a "salaried employee" as we prefer to say today) means being deprived of the greatest part of your life's effort, and of any control over what you do, still more why you do it. At least you have a job, keep quiet and be content. Buy something. The effort you make at work is something foreign to you, something you do when you are not free, precisely when you are under the constraint of hired labour, of work.

Is it not an immense privilege to fix yourself an aim, and to bend all your faculties to that aim, to live it sensually, that is to say through every one of the physical senses, both internal and external? For most of the time, foreign aims are fixed for us, or worse still, we adopt as our own, aims that do not belong to us.

Is it not an absurdity to separate the mind and the body? We talk of "manual" and "intellectual" labour, as if manual work could be done without engaging the mind, and as if intellectual work could be done by a disembodied brain. This way of seeing things is precisely the expression of a world where the human being is deprived of its real being, where its own powers are stripped from it, to the point where we feel most free when we are least human, that is to say the least engaged in a collective social effort. But this effort is foreign to us because it does not belong to us, so that we only feel free when we are reduced to the state of a passive "consumer". Of course, we need moments of ease and relaxation too. But when these are reserved for our private lives, while our essential effort is reserved for the domain of unfreedom which is work, then our private lives are deprived of meaning.

The point here is not to moralise about "effort". Morality has nothing to do with it. If I return to my experience of the Way, the need for effort seems obvious. The moments that affected me most powerfully present themselves in my mind's eye: the moment of exaltation when at last I spied the Pyrenees; the physical and mental euphoria acquired after weeks of walking; the moment of transcendance experienced on the heights of *Los Ospedales*; even the feeling of melancholy that gripped me by the ocean near Fisterra. Nothing of all that would have come to me from a mere Sunday walk. Mind and body are so intimately linked, so necessary one to the other, that such mental sensations are only possible through physical training. This is hardly original, the Taoists knew this long before I did. But you must live it truly to understand it.

Fortunate indeed am I to have lived the Way! For weeks I have driven my body on. I have suffered its fatigue and its injuries (happily, only small ones), but I have also felt its joy, the joy brought by this intoxicating sensation that the whole is working perfectly, that every part of the body plays its part in this living being that is my self, in all its complexity, in this almost miraculous result of millions of years of evolution. I have been able to see, not just passively with the eyes but actively, sensually, with the whole body in movement. I have had time to think, but the Way also allowed my mind to wander and let the unconscious work — these pages are in part the result. I have been able to talk to many people, or rather, I have been able to listen, and I am the richer for what others have given me of their lives and their thoughts. I thank them all, even those who got on my nerves at times.

So I come to the end of my journey. And the end, after all, is always a new beginning.